TESTIMONIALS

"Coaching" is a term that can be hard to define. It often means different things to different people. This book offers a solid system for defining "coaching" and for implementing it in a variety of different situations. It is both very detailed and structured in a way that makes it easy to follow. I think it could be a very useful guide for any helping professional."

- Dr. Daniel C. Marston, Ph.D., ABPP
Clinical Psychologist
Author "Comparative Psychology For Clinical Psychologists And Therapists: What Studying Animal Behavior Tells Us About Human Psychology"

"The life of a busy entrepreneur doesn't leave much time for error or wasted investment of time. When we need to be at optimal performance level, we need our strategies and solutions to be consumable and implementable NOW! The authors of The MindCoach System have done just that — served up a simple protocol to help EVERY reader to live life more effectively — even those that hardly have a minute to spare!"

- Dr. Sage Breslin, Ph.D.
Transformation Psychologist
Best-Selling Author "Breaking Through: The Conscious Leader's and Entrepreneur's Guide to Amplify Intuition, Clarity, Vision, Motivation and Productivity"

"Over the past 20 years of practicing medicine, the one thing I've learned is that there is nothing I can do as a doctor more powerful than preventing an illness or injury. The MindCoach System is similar and uses scientifically validated principles to help the reader achieve their goals. It is especially effective because anybody can force themselves to do something one time, but you need a system to do the right thing every time. I highly recommend physicians and healthcare professionals use this system to help their patients understand the principles to achieve consistent results in life."

- Dr. Timothy Dancy, M.D.
Orthopedic Surgeon
Assistant Professor in the Department of Orthopaedic Surgery at the University of Pittsburgh

---

"The tools and strategies in this book have helped me grow my business and improve my mindset. The MindCoach System trains your unconscious mind so that you can improve your thought patterns and push through upper limits. Once we break through the mental barriers, we can achieve our highest potential."

- Theresa Nicole, RDN
Transformational Nutrition Coach
Author "Food Detox for Weight Loss & Food Cravings"

"There are many great books out there that can help us to improve ourselves. Some of them help with goal setting. Others help with health or finances. Others help with specific psychological issues, time management, or certain occupations and industries. However, few (if any) of them take a whole-life approach to personal transformation. MindCoach is different. This system demystifies the process of personal growth and development by getting to the core of what drives us, what guides us to success, and what gets in our way. It teaches the reader simple methods of self-mastery that can lead to a new level of clarity and control."

- Dr. Sean Elliot Martin, Ph.D.

Assistant Professor, Program Director, Martial Arts Grandmaster

Intelligence Studies Program at Point Park University. Author "Doing Good Works, Small Acts That Make A Big Difference" and "Structuralist Methods Of Psy Op Target Analysis, A Supplemental Manual."

"I really appreciated how you incorporated multiple ways to think through something. It felt like a glossary for difficult situations. I can turn to your book and find a beneficial way to get to a solution. I think your book would help me set attainable goals and remind me to be kind to myself during the journey."

- Kate Gustaferro

College Student

B.S. Psychology and Childhood Studies at the University Miami Ohio

THE MINDCOACH SYSTEM

A Scientifically Proven 7-Step Process To Unlock Your Peak Potential

THE MINDCOACH SYSTEM

*A Scientifically Proven 7-Step Process
To Unlock Your Peak Potential*

ADAM KRIPKE

&

DAVID LOSHELDER

The MindCoach System

Copyright © 2021 Adam Kripke and David Loshelder

All rights reserved. No part of this book may be reproduced or transmitted in any form or by any means, electronic or mechanical, including photocopying, recording, or by any information storage and retrieval system, without permission in writing from the authors.

ISBN: 978-1-946702-50-0

Published by Freeze Time Media

Cover design by Adam Kripke

DISCLAIMER

THIS PROGRAM IS FOR EDUCATIONAL PURPOSES ONLY. THIS IS NOT A BUSINESS OPPORTUNITY. NO INCOME OPPORTUNITY IS BEING PRESENTED IN THIS BOOK. WE MAKE NO PROMISES OR GUARANTEES THAT YOU WILL GET THE SAME OR SIMILAR RESULTS OR ANY RESULT AT ALL. ANY EXAMPLES PROVIDED DURING THIS BOOK ARE NOT TO BE INTERPRETED AS ANY GUARANTEE, PROMISE, REPRESENTATION AND/OR ASSURANCE. WE DO NOT PURPORT OUR BUSINESS AND/OR US AS BEING A "GET RICH SCHEME" AND WE DO NOT OFFER ANY LEGAL, MEDICAL, TAX, OR OTHER PROFESSIONAL ADVICE. UNDERSTAND THAT WITH ANY PERSONAL AND/OR BUSINESS ENDEAVOR THERE IS AN INHERENT RISK, INCLUDING A LOSS OF CAPITAL AND LOSS OF CUSTOMERS, AND THEREFORE YOU ASSUME ALL RESPONSIBILITY FOR ANY SUCH RISK.

YOUR SUCCESS DEPENDS ENTIRELY ON YOUR OWN EFFORT, MOTIVATION, COMMITMENT AND FOLLOW-THROUGH. WE CANNOT PREDICT AND WE DO NOT GUARANTEE THAT YOU WILL ATTAIN A PARTICULAR RESULT, AND YOU ACCEPT AND UNDERSTAND THAT RESULTS DIFFER FOR EACH INDIVIDUAL. EACH INDIVIDUAL'S RESULTS DEPEND ON HIS OR HER UNIQUE BACKGROUND, DEDICATION, DESIRE, MOTIVATION, ACTIONS, AND NUMEROUS OTHER FACTORS. BY CONTINUING TO READ, YOU ACKNOWLEDGE THAT YOU FULLY AGREE THAT THERE ARE NO GUARANTEES AS TO THE SPECIFIC OUTCOME OR RESULTS YOU CAN EXPECT FROM USING THE INFORMATION YOU RECEIVE ON OR THROUGH THIS BOOK OR PRODUCT.

THE CONTENT IS NOT INTENDED TO BE A SUBSTITUTE FOR PROFESSIONAL MEDICAL ADVICE, DIAGNOSIS, OR TREATMENT. ALWAYS SEEK THE ADVICE OF YOUR PHYSICIAN OR OTHER QUALIFIED HEALTH PROVIDER WITH ANY QUESTIONS YOU MAY HAVE REGARDING A MEDICAL CONDITION. IN CASE OF SEVERE ISSUES OR SUICIDAL THOUGHTS, CONTACT A QUALIFIED HEALTH PROFESSIONAL.

To anyone who is striving to

reach their full potential

ACKNOWLEDGMENTS

This book was made possible by the support and encouragement of the following people:

A special thanks goes to the following people who helped with the creation of this book: Sean Elliot Martin, Ph.D., and our publisher, Di Freeze, whose suggestions and creativity made this book a published work for all to read; the list continues with the people that were a great influence and offered so much to this book ... and to anyone who strives to take control of their life.

TABLE OF CONTENTS

TESTIMONIALS	i
DISCLAIMER	ix
ACKNOWLEDGMENTS	xiii
OUR DREAM	xvii
WHAT IS THE MINDCOACH SYSTEM?	1
YOUR MIND MATTERS	7
THE QUALITIES OF A GREAT COACH	11
BE YOUR OWN COACH	13
HOW TO USE THE MINDCOACH SYSTEM	17
DREAMS	21
WHY	29
GOALS	35
STRATEGY	47
EXECUTION	63
THE B.E.T.A. CYCLE	81
BELIEFS	85
EMOTIONS	88
THOUGHTS	95
ACTIONS	100
THE MIND'S EYE & THE BETA CYCLE	104
E.S.P.	108
THE 3A's	115
CREATE SEPARATION	123
6 TOOLS FOR MIND COACHING	125
DISCOVER YOUR B.E.T.A.	136
PEAK POTENTIAL	151

CONCLUSION	157
THE MINDCOACH SYSTEM WORKBOOK	161
ABOUT THE AUTHORS	205
CONTACT INFORMATION	209
MINDCOACH SYSTEM PROGRAMS	211
MINDCOACH PRODUCTS AND APPAREL	215
LEADERSHIP ACCELERATOR CERTIFICATION COURSE	217
DISC PERSONALITY ASSESSMENTS	219
OTHER BOOKS	221

OUR DREAM

To help individuals achieve and maintain their full potential in life and business.

WHAT IS THE MINDCOACH SYSTEM?

The MindCoach System is a comprehensive success system that both guides and coaches you on how to live at your full potential. The system provides you with scientifically proven tools to design a road map to reach your goals, as well as simple exercises to identify and overcome the overwhelming mental barriers that hinder your motivation and confidence in your life.

We MUST learn how to coach our own minds. Uncontrolled, our minds can create hell on earth out of thin air. Our minds can conjure up all sorts of unfounded fears, insecurities, and emotions that can leave us crippled under the weight of its invisible forces. The mind can be unrelenting, brutal, and deceptive. Worst of all, many times we believe what it is telling us and never think to question whether or not these thoughts and emotions are really true. It's time to take back control, and this is why The MindCoach System was designed.

Losing is unavoidable. It will find you no matter how careful, calculated, truthful, or stoic you are. What really matters is how you deal with failure in your mind, how you treat other people, and how you use failure as fuel to grow and become more. All highly successful people failed at some point in their lives. These losses, however, become overshadowed by their successes.

Several years ago, I went through multiple devastating experiences all at once. I lost hundreds of thousands of dollars in a real estate investment, my mentor and business partner of 10+ years developed early onset Alzheimer's, another business partner was diagnosed with a brain tumor for the third time, a contractor stole from me and ended up doing five years in prison, my parents had an unforeseen financial crisis, one of my closest friends passed away, and my family life was on the rocks. Without going into too much detail, this was by far the most painful time in my life to date. Life was happening and it wasn't kind. In fact, it conjured up some of the most visceral negative emotional responses I've ever experienced in my life. The pain was unbearable. It wasn't physical pain; it manifested in the form of depression and a sense of feeling stupid, unworthy, less than, and "not a good businessman." It paralyzed me from taking new risks, seeking new opportunities, and even enjoying the time with my family. I hated waking up and could feel the pressure weighing on my chest as I got out of bed. All I could think about was my loss, the people I disappointed, the people that failed me, what I could do differently, and none of it helped. It became a vicious, self-destructive, repetitive cycle that never seemed to resolve despite the things I tried.

When you reach that unfathomable level of anger, frustration, and self-loathing, it completely cripples you mentally. Your quality of life changes into a toxic mess for days, weeks, months, and sometimes years. I needed a way out. After seeking the help of gurus, mentors, books, friends, and family, none of them had the all-in-one solution. I tried speaking with other close friends and family about my troubles, but no one had an answer. And worse, after putting myself out there, some even distanced themselves from me like I was contagious with some highly infectious "failure disease." It was more complex than just singing "Kumbaya" and jumping up and down saying "yes I can." Nothing was working.… I read countless books, attended seminars, sat with professionals, and nothing worked. None of them had a checklist, a system, or a comprehensive process to fix everything. None of them had all the pieces of the puzzle. Some would have tools to reignite your desire to win, some had methods to set new and exciting goals, others showed how to create a short-cut to your seemingly unattainable dreams, and some would talk about ways to conquer your mind, but none had an all-in-one system. Actually, what I learned was that all of these things, in fact, must work together in harmony to turn your life around. I realized everything is connected and I started a mission to figure it out. I never wanted to go through the same mental anguish ever again. I started on a personal journey to design a system that made sense and was easy to follow, a system that could get you back on track when the shit really hits the fan.

At this time, I was collaborating on a few projects with David Loshelder and, as we began to share our trials and tribulations of life, I realized (to my surprise) that we had a similar mission. Together, David and I cracked the code and *The MindCoach System* was born.

The MindCoach System is based on years of neuroscience research and is a fusion of some of the best performance systems that exist today. All the individual exercises utilized are backed by sound scholarly data. These exercises were constructed to give individuals the power to take back control of their minds, even in some of the most challenging scenarios. This program is meant to be simple and to the point. There are many other ways to accomplish the pieces of the puzzle here but, for the sake of simplicity, we extracted the most proven and powerful systems available. If you are looking for a simple and complete A to Z system to permanently manage the ups and downs in your life, then this is the only tool that I know of that does it.

For those of you currently going through tough times, or that are experiencing something similar to what David and I went through, I hope and pray this MindCoach System brings you the same level of love, comfort, and empowerment that it brought to us.

One would think that the skills to handle the common stresses of life would be taught in schools or by our parents or mentors, but that is not necessarily true. Unless you seek professional help, or read piles of books, or study practical psychology, your chances of being able to control your unconscious mind are practically nonexistent. The MindCoach System was created because I realized that something was missing from the countless inspirational books and recordings of self-help gurus. Occasionally, their suggestions brought temporary or partial answers, but none had one cohesive solution that you could understand at a glance. After you understand the elements of The MindCoach System, just looking at the MindCoach Pyramid will bring you clarity. You will know where you are and what is stopping you.

This system was developed because it takes virtually everything into account. Most systems focus on one aspect of life, but do not explain how they tie together to create your destiny. Most licensed professionals jump around from tool to tool, treating the symptoms as they go, but they are unable to identify and provide a comprehensive solution. You will find that, no matter what internal or external barrier you face, The MindCoach System will help you identify, assess, and ultimately overcome it.

What we are presenting here represents a compilation of decades of research, information gleaned from numerous sources and the insights and methods of many highly trained performance coaches and doctors. After careful investigation, my team and I drew conclusions as to what strategies worked best and combined them into one "simple to use tool" to help people regain control of their lives. We represent this tool in a simple pyramid. Every level of the pyramid serves as a foundation for the pieces above it, creating a solid and aesthetically appealing structure. Each level builds upon the last, creating a harmonious relationship all the way from identifying your true purpose to becoming your highest and best self. Some people call it "the zone," some people call it "flow," and others call it "your full potential." Completing the exercises associated with each level of the pyramid will challenge you. You will have to confront your unconscious mind and question some of the beliefs, values, and thoughts you hold most dear. You will begin to recognize inefficiencies in the way you live and find new ways to overcome the barriers in your life.

So, who is this program really for? The answer is simple, truly everyone. Whether you are a fortune 500 CEO, an entrepreneur, an employee, a mother, a teenager, or an athlete, you will receive massive benefits from this program. Now you will finally have a simple yet comprehensive visual tool to guide you and keep you on track, to make sense of the action or inaction you are taking to reach your goals. Print off the visual tool and hang it on your wall, keep a completed copy next to you during the day, review it in the morning and before bed, and fill it out again when you need to update any of the components of the pyramid. This tool will help you to address the limiting unconscious thoughts you have, the emotions you feel, the behaviors you exhibit, and even your core values and beliefs. With the right questions provided in this program, you can dig in and overcome some of the most challenging times you will ever encounter. This program will be your guide to designing your ultimate self.

YOUR MIND MATTERS

"An enormous portion of cognitive activity is non-conscious, figuratively speaking, it could be 99 percent; we probably will never know precisely how much is outside awareness."

- Dr. Emanuel Donchin,
Director of the Laboratory for Cognitive Psychophysiology at the University of Illinois

Our minds are under attack. According to the American Marketing Association, the average person is exposed to 4,000 to 10,000 branded messages each and every day. And guess what ... the number of distractions you face daily will continue to grow over the rest of your lifetime. Less than a decade ago, the number of distractions inundating us was a fraction of what it is today. Everyone and everything is constantly competing for your attention, your time, and your money, and guess what ... they are winning. (You already said guess what in this paragraph. Maybe think of another phrase so it's not redundant.)

In today's society, we lose precious hours communicating on social media, browsing Facebook, watching the next Netflix TV series, or being subjected to 24-hour news sources intent on bombarding us with facts and images related to pandemics, civil unrest, and natural disasters.

The media thrives on showing us what we should look like, what we should buy, and what we are missing in our lives.

It evokes primal emotions such as shock and fear to grab

our attention. And yet, we let it invade our minds without a fight. There are three things that attack your unconscious mind, planting seeds of depression, anxiety, fear, low self-esteem, and sometimes even disease. Without the right psychological tools to cut through the bullshit, the world heavily influences how we think, feel, behave, and believe. *Everything* we see, hear and even touch can trigger physiological responses deep within our unconscious mind without us even knowing it.

So, what can you do to regain control of your mind? You must have a way to fight back and regain the life you deserve. The only way to accomplish this is to have at your disposal the exercises and tools to become aware of, assess, and ultimately take the action necessary to redirect and correct your behaviors and actions.

There are only 3 factors that influence your mind. These factors are the environment, other people, and yourself. Think for a moment about the effect that the environment, the people around you, and your own uncontrolled thoughts have on your performance in life and business. The impact these can have on your performance can be tremendous. Later in the program, we will go into more detail on these 3 factors, but for now let's look at their potential effects. Notice how many of these you may be experiencing right now. Here are just some of the lasting effects that may go unnoticed:

- Low self-esteem
- Lowered expectations
- Sub-par performance
- Emotional roller coaster rides
- Increased anger and frustration
- Undesired reactions

- Excuses to cover up poor performance
- Lack of motivation
- Unfounded beliefs
- Habits and behaviors that you do but don't know why
- Regular thoughts that stop your progress
- And the list goes on and on…

Considering that the vast majority of mental activities are hidden from our conscious attention, don't you think this might be worth understanding a bit more? How to coach your own mind is not taught in schools, yet studies by numerous cognitive neuroscientists conclude that only 5% of our cognitive activities (decisions, emotions, actions, behavior) are conscious, whereas the remaining 95% is generated in a non-conscious manner. For years, I never knew this function of our brain even existed, and yet it has some serious side effects in our daily lives. Once you become conscious of this activity happening in the background, it becomes easier to become aware of, assess, and take action to coach your mind back on track. Soon, you will have the power to question the previously unquestionable and create breakthrough results from taking back control from your own unconscious mind.

THE QUALITIES OF A GREAT COACH

"A coach is someone who tells you what you don't want to hear, who has you see what you don't want to see, so you can be who you have always known you could be."

-Tom Landry,
Professional American Football Coach

Can you remember a coach who made a positive impact on you? What qualities did they have? How did they help to push you, inspire you, or support you when times got tough? Coaches come in many forms, from your parents to your schoolteachers, to your mentors. They may have helped you learn how to swing a bat, throw a ball, run, swim, or any other sporting event you might have been involved in at that time. However, with great coaching comes more than just learning techniques and skills — much more. Great coaches inspire and build self-esteem and values. They teach mental fortitude, fair play, respect for yourself and others, and many other factors that make you a better individual.

Coaches push you to want more and be more and take you to higher levels than what you believed you could reach when you started. They can see things that you cannot and help you to recognize what may need to change to up your game. The best aspect about great coaches is how they give you these experiences and skills to take with you for the rest of your life. With practice, over time, you become an upgraded version of yourself. If your coach did their job well, you developed the skills to not only continue to coach yourself but also share your knowledge and experience with others.

This program is designed to be your coach. It will help you find your blind spots and give you the exercises, motivation, and insights you need to reach your full potential in life and business. Each section of this program has scientifically proven exercises that will set the building blocks to your future self. The goal is to prepare you with a comprehensive system and simple exercises to allow you to coach yourself to the life you deserve. Once you learn and implement these strategies and techniques, you will be able to overcome the barriers that have stopped you from reaching the top.

BE YOUR OWN COACH

"A great coach can lead you to a place where you don't need him anymore."

- Andre Agassi,
Professional Tennis Player and 1996 Olympic Gold Medalist

Many years ago, I attended a national judo training camp in Colorado Springs, Colorado. I spent most of my summer training twice a day with the nation's best competitors and coaches, and the paces we were put through were the most challenging I had faced since I began practicing judo. The top instructor held a seventh-degree black belt and guided our advanced training that summer. A pioneer in American judo and martial arts, Phil Porter was one of the greatest coaches of the day.

During our three-hour training sessions, Porter would intersperse his philosophies of commitment, mindfulness, attitude, perspective, and life throughout our workouts while he punished us with exercise, drills, and hundreds of repetitions. Porter's intelligence was obvious, his charisma contagious, and his leadership legendary. He demanded excellence and unwavering commitment from all the students. He commanded that we focus intensely every session on the tasks and drills he introduced. In one of our many long, grueling sessions, he showed a millisecond of mercy (or, at least that is how it appeared) when he stopped our training and began to speak to us in a serious, passionate tone.

He said, "During these intensive training sessions, you will have moments of doubt and despair in which you will think you cannot go on." He then said something that I have never forgotten: "You are your best coach."

"Champions coach themselves. So, practice, strive, and learn to coach yourself. The best coach is you!" Porter proclaimed.

A champion is what I wanted to become. My ultimate goal was to become ranked #1 in the U.S.A. in my respective weight class. Armed with the realization that "I am my own best coach" and with the goal of becoming the best, I marked out my plan of attack to reach that goal of being one of the country's best judokas.

I was 16 years old at the time when he said those words, and I do not believe I will ever forget them. I have played that decree hundreds of thousands of times in my mind since then.

I realized very quickly that being my own coach was much harder than I thought. I said to myself, how do you coach yourself? What do you say to yourself? What should I be believing, thinking, and feeling? I understood the training regiments and followed the protocols of training from my instructors. I attended the required training sessions, followed the conditioning and strength training workouts, and adhered to a strict diet plan. Since that was subscribed for me, what did Porter mean by me being my own coach? Even though I was training hard, I still wondered what *the difference was* between the champion and everyone else. When you compete at the national level as I did, everyone trains hard. Everyone is in tip-top shape. Everyone's diet is dialed in to play at the highest levels. Since all the top national players were practicing about the same number of hours, training about the same, and eating about the same, what made the first-place winner different from second, third or fourth place losers?

As I pondered the notion of Porter's self-coaching proclamation, the revelation of mental strategy and discipline came into my focus. Coaching is all a mental strategy. Through my research in performance psychology and interviewing top athletes, I found that they all have a system of thinking that keeps them motivated, positive, hopeful, confident, and mentally tough. This was the X-factor for me, and I was determined to find it and capture that number one spot!

Over the course of a few years, and applying what I learned, I did reach the number one spot in the country in my respective weight class. I was always close but once I applied the mental strategies of top performers, I found my confidence and mental toughness increased tenfold. This is where The MindCoach System can help you. We have created a system that takes the trial and error out of the equation. The profundity of The MindCoach System will give you the autonomy to think like a champion. You will have the competitive edge in life. This comprehensive platform gives you the road map, the tools, and the process to coach your mind, emotions, and your body in ways that arm you with a keen sense of mental acuity and focus to march you directly towards your goals. This is the "coach" in The MindCoach System. Now let's take a look at the nuts and bolts of this exciting program to start your journey towards success, happiness, and winning.

- David Loshelder

HOW TO USE THE MINDCOACH SYSTEM

Each of the following chapters will provide you with an explanation, supporting research, and examples of how that particular level may be impacting your performance. The chapters start with the foundation of the pyramid, identifying your "Dreams," and then coaching you through all of the other necessary layers to reach the top of the pyramid, your "Peak Potential." Each level of the pyramid is critical and all must be completed to reach your desired outcome. At the end of the book we included a complete set of exercises accompanying each level of the pyramid. The carefully designed exercises will coach you through the entire process end to end. Not only will this process demystify the path to achieving peak potential, but it also provides a reusable tool to reach your peak potential in both life and business.

1) DREAMS
2) WHY
3) GOALS
4) STRATEGY
5) EXECUTION
6) BETA CYCLE
7) PEAK POTENTIAL

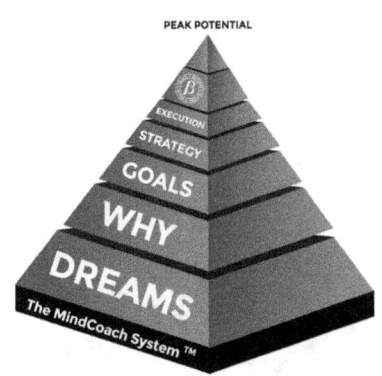

NOTE: It is both natural and expected for your pyramid to change and evolve over time. To account for this, revisit and update the MindCoach Workbook as often as necessary to remain current with your present focus.

Let's jump right into the first step
in The MindCoach System.

Step 1: Dreams

DREAMS

What Do You Dream About?

DREAMS

"Nothing happens unless we first dream."

- Carl Sandburg,
*American Poet, Biographer, Journalist,
and 3 Time Pulitzer Prize Winner*

Have you ever heard of someone dreaming of winning the lottery? I'm sure you have. Maybe even you? According to the legendary Austrian neurologist and founder of psychoanalysis, Sigmund Freud, dreams are imagery of a wish or impulse from childhood that has since been repressed. He believed that dreams revealed repressed conflicts or wishes. Today, most scientists don't agree with Freud's view of dreams, but they do agree that dreams may be our unconscious sorting out the thoughts of our day. The content and purpose of dreams are not fully understood, even though it has been a topic of scientific, philosophical, and religious interest throughout human history.

Everything that has and will ever be created by mankind started as a dream, a figment of the imagination that, with the appropriate action, was born into reality. Albert Einstein was one of the greatest daydreamers of all time. In school, young Einstein would stare out of the window and daydream about how light traveled. It is widely reported that all great creators, from Einstein discovering spacetime to Thomas Edison creating the incandescent light bulb to Steve Jobs creating the iPhone to Elon Musk creating reusable rockets, all had one thing in common: their innate instinct to dream. Carl Sandburg wrote, "Nothing happens unless we first dream." The human mind gives us the unique ability to consciously dream our reality into existence. Dreaming is an incredible tool that the human mind has at its disposal. As far as we know, we are the only species that can think about something, dream about it, and make it happen in a very specific way.

So, let me ask you a question … what do you dream about? Have you ever dreamt of lying comfortably on the beach holding a cold beverage and listening to the waves on your favorite Caribbean island? Or maybe you dreamt of a salesman handing over the keys to your new, shiny, fire-red Mustang GT convertible. Or maybe you dreamt of holding your beautiful newborn baby. As you dream about this succession of images, ideas, and notions, you connect with the emotions and sensations in your mind and drift in and out of a daydream state thinking, wishing, and visualizing what you want in life. These dreams can elicit feelings that can both inspire or scare us. When designing our life without a dream that inspires us, there is no map. There is no direction. There is no destination to move towards. In this section, we will help you to explore and expand your dreams.

Don't worry, you don't need to be perfect or get this exactly right out of the gate. You need to start somewhere, and your first try will not be perfect. This system is designed in such a way to allow you to update, change, or modify your answers in the future. As you progress through life, the opportunities you have available to you will change, people in your life will change, and your goals and dreams may change. Life will change, and that's OK. When this happens, your application of The MindCoach System must change with it.

DREAM EXERCISES

1. DREAM STORMING

The first action in the Dream Storming process is for you to think about what you want to become, what you want to do, and what you want to have in your life or business. In this step you will imagine your future. Do your best to write down as much as possible, and be as concise as possible. Focus on writing down dreams that truly excite you and that elicit powerful positive emotions when you think about them. Do not limit yourself. Stretch your mind and think of things you want that are outside of your comfort zone. Set a timer for 15 minutes and write down as much as you can. And most importantly, HAVE FUN!

Dream Storming will discover and define your ultimate dream life and is a visual exercise that turns your mental imagination into reality. When you are Dream Storming, it will have a profound effect on your subconscious mind that subsequently clarifies and focuses you on what you want in life. Our brains now see physical representations of where we want to go and subconsciously help us to find ways to get there. Dream Storming is intended to activate your Reticular Activating System (RAS). Having these images as a reference is a great way to help them remain in the forefront of your mind to help pull you in the direction of your desired future.

*NOTE: On the next page is a list of categories to help you expand upon your dreams.

10 CATEGORIES OF LIFE

Family and Home

What does your dream house look like? Where is it located?
What does your family life look like?

Recreation and fun

Where would you travel for vacation?
What activities would you do more of?

Personal Growth

If you were to aim even higher, what does that dream look like for you?
What have you dreamed of learning or doing in your life?

Physical Health/Self-image

What do you want to look like?
What does a healthy lifestyle look like to you?

Spiritual

What does your spirituality look like to you?
How would you like to practice your spirituality?

Work & Career

If you could do anything and couldn't fail, what would you do?
What would you do for work?
What would you invest your time in?

Financial/Wealth

How much money would you have? What would you do with it?
Where would you invest your money?

Social Life

Who would you spend your time with?
What types of people would you love to be around?

Legacy

What does your legacy look like?

Contribution

Who or what would you support?

2. CREATE YOUR DREAM BOARD

Let's now turn your dreams into reality! In this exercise you will be creating a dream board. Your job now is to find 25 images that communicate and depict your ultimate dream life. You can use any medium you want to get this done. Take pictures, cut out magazine pages, or download images from the internet. Dream Storming™ is a visual exercise that turns your imagination into reality. By participating in this activity, you will find it has a profound effect on our subconscious mind that subsequently clarifies and focuses on what you want in life. When we do this, our brains now see where we want to go and help us to find ways to get there. We have just activated the Reticular Activating System (RAS) — but more on this later. Having these images as a reference is a great way to help them remain in the forefront of your mind. However, sticking these in a drawer will not get the job done. These must become a constant reminder. You may have heard the saying "Out of sight out of mind." Well, the only way to keep your dreams in your subconscious mind is to regularly view these images to keep your mind sharp and ready to figure out paths to reach your dreams.

Here are a few suggestions to keep these images in view:

- **VISION BOARD** - Print off your images and paste or pin them onto a wall or cork board that remains in constant view.
- **DREAM BOOK** - Create a small scrapbook or photo album that you can look at often. This can be in either paper or digital form.
- **BACKGROUND IMAGES** - Take your images and turn them into your digital background on any of your digital devices.

- **SCREENSAVER** - Save all your images into a folder on your computer or digital device called "Dream Board." Next, go to your screensaver setting and make these images appear as your screensaver. Voila! Now you have an ongoing reminder of where you want to go.
- **SHARE WITH FRIENDS** - Create an album online or share these powerful images with your friends on social media.
- **CREATE A VIDEO** - Turn your images into a compelling video presentation. Watch this video often to keep your dreams top of mind.

Let's move to the next step in The MindCoach System.

Step 2: Why

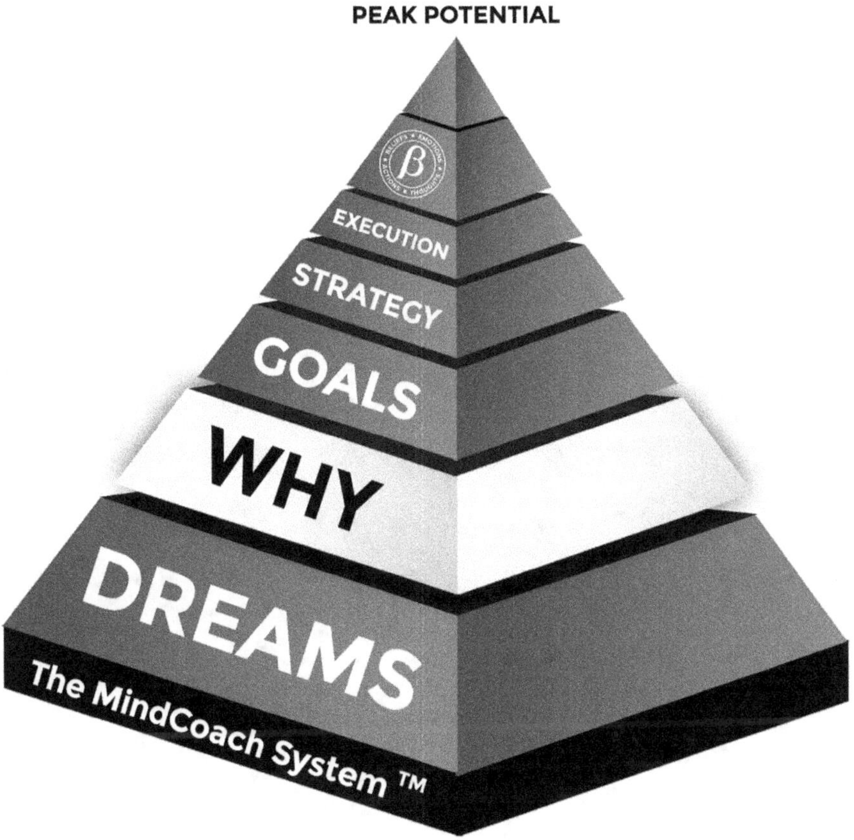

WHY

Why Do You REALLY Want It?

WHY

"There are two great days in a person's life — the day we are born and the day we discover why."

- William Barclay,
Famous Scottish Scholar

"Research by Bain & Company concludes that if a satisfied employee's productivity level is 100%, an engaged employee's level is 144%, but the productivity level of an employee that is truly inspired by the purpose of their employer is a whopping 225%." - (Bain & Company 2015)

"If employees feel they are working towards a good cause, it can increase their productivity by up to 30%." - (LMU Center for Economic Studies 2014)

Your WHY is the fuel that generates the reasons you take action, and your actions are directly proportional to your success. Without a purpose, why would you do anything? After analyzing your actions, you will discover you really do not do anything for "no reason."

Let me give you an example: I said to my son the other day, "Let's go get some ice cream."

He said, "Why are we getting ice cream?" To this day not sure why he asked, but I said, "No reason, let's just go get some ice cream."

However, there were, in fact, many reasons, as I thought about it later. One: is that I wanted to spend time with my son. Two: is that I have a sweet tooth for ice cream. Three: is that I worked hard that day and wanted to reward myself. As you can see, even a simple action has many reasons, or "whys," driving it.

People contend that they don't know their "why" or can't find their "why," yet in actuality, many know the actions they need to take to succeed. By working backwards, you can better define or attach a strong "why" to the subsequent action you need to take. This can help you discover the correct "why" and then marry it to the appropriate action.

Some reasons are easier to identify than others, but in time you will come up with a reason, good or bad. I recall watching a documentary featuring U.S. Navy SEALs and the grueling training they undergo to become elite warriors. In one training session, a recruit was on the verge of giving up and quitting the training. You could see the anguish on this young man's face as the drill instructor mercilessly berated and castigated him. The instructor, while trying everything to motivate this soldier to continue the brutal exercise, said something that exemplifies the importance of having a "why" when he screamed at the struggling young man, "JUST FIND AN EXCUSE TO WIN!" In an instant, I saw this man's face change from absolute despair to damning determination. It was like a switch that was flipped, and the young man found the fire, inspiration, and ability within himself to complete the training session. This is the power of finding a reason to win and knowing why you are doing something important. The next time you want to quit something that is difficult, you need to "find an excuse to win!"

PEEL BACK THE LAYERS

The Seven Layer Exercise helps you to peel back the layers and dig deeper into discovering your "reason to win." It helps you mobilize a powerful engine that will propel you through tough times. You need to find a true purpose that generates a strong emotional shock of desire to achieve. On the surface you may desire a bigger house, or perhaps you strive to make people happy, or maybe you simply need to prove to yourself you can do it. Though these goals have merit, in truth they do not address the real underpinnings of your efforts. Take time to really ponder these questions to learn the more compelling "why" that will become the foundation of your MindCoach Pyramid. The exercise below is simple but profound and a crucial step towards realizing your full potential.

EXERCISE: Discover Your Why, The 7-Layer Exercise "Peeling Back The Layers"

What is your dream?

1. What is important to you about realizing this dream?
2. Why is that important to you?
3. Why is that important to you?
4. Why is that important to you?
5. Why is that important to you?
6. Why is that important to you?
7. Why is that important to you?

EXAMPLE

What is your dream? ***I want to run the Boston marathon***

1. What is important to you about realizing this dream? ***I want to prove to myself I can do it.***
2. Why is that important to you? ***I want to complete one before I get too old.***
3. Why is that important to you? ***I don't want to regret not doing a marathon.***
4. Why is that important to you? ***I want to feel like I made my life count and I lived my life to its fullest.***
5. Why is that important to you? ***I want to experience everything life has to offer.***
6. Why is that important to you? ***I don't want to be old and feel like I could have done more with my life.***
7. Why is that important to you? ***I want to die without any regrets.***

The final answer you come up with will then roll over into the next level of the pyramid where we set your goal. Your final "why" will be used to add more power and motivation to the goal you create.

Let's move to the next step in The MindCoach System.

Step 3: Goals

GOALS

What Goals Do You Need To Set To Accomplish It?

GOALS

"Set the kind of goals that will make something of you to achieve them."

- Jim Rohn,
American Entrepreneur, Author and Motivational Speaker

Where will you be in ten years? Let's say you decide to take a sailboat out into the open ocean and raise the sails. The wind will push you. It may take you into the eye of a hurricane, it may take you to a tropical paradise, or it may take you to the middle of nowhere to die a gruesome death. This is a metaphor for not having goals. It's like taking your hands off the steering wheel and letting destiny have its way with you. Setting goals is a way to build a roadmap to your desired destination. You may or may not actually arrive, but you will undoubtedly be closer by setting goals than you will be by letting life push you where it sees fit.

> A Harvard Business study revealed that 83% of the population does not have goals, 14% have a plan in mind, but are unwritten goals, and 3% have goals written down. The study went on to find that the 14% who have goals are 10x times more successful than those without goals. The 3% with written goals are 3x times more successful than the 14% with unwritten goals.

We often hear the elderly lamenting over what they did not do in life when they had the opportunity. Staring into the past and looking at the things you never accomplished is like having an itch that you can't scratch. Knowing that you could have done more, done it better, or done something different to change your current outcome is haunting. Because you cannot change the past, the pain of "what might have been" is relentless. All the decisions you make along the way build into a crescendo towards the end of life. One of the ways to stave off regrets is to consciously decide where you are going. Taking control of your destiny provides a road map to your goals. You may need to encounter an occasional detour or roadblock, but knowing you are traveling in the right direction reassures you that you are still on the right path. Even though you may eventually alter your destination, you should find comfort knowing this change was made consciously, based on evidence and circumstances and not out of fear of the attempt. Designing the life you desire starts with creating goals worth striving for, goals that excite you, challenge you, and lead you to your ultimate destination.

Many wise people have stated that your dreams do not become reality until you have a reason for them, and your goals cannot be mobilized until you have a date set for their achievement. So far in this program, you have defined your dream and created the "why" for that dream. Now it is time to take those two elements and make them into a meaningful and measurable goal!

Let's take a look at how you will do this.

First, you will take one of your dreams from the "Dream" section and make that the subject of your goal. Second, you want to declare what you will do, get, or want from the dream. This is an essential part of the goals statement because it gives you the specific action orientation you will need to work on your goal. This will tell you what to do, the actions you will take to accomplish your goal. Third, you will place a date that you expect your goals to be reached. Placing a deadline on the goals will give you the ability to design strategies and timetables for certain benchmarks to track your progress toward your goal. Fourth, you will implant the reason from the "Why" section into the goal. By adding the reason into the goal statement, this will give you the motivation and energy to work toward your goal.

In the next part of the system is the strategy section, in which you will begin to design strategies to help you reach the goal with more accuracy and certainty.

In The MindCoach System, we have developed an acrostic for you to use when developing a goal statement. The acrostic is spelled D.I.B.B.S. and it stands for the following listed below:

DIBBS - (**D**REAMS - **I** WILL - **B**Y - **B**ECAUSE - **S**TRATEGY)

D: Dreams (the dream I have in my life)
I: I will (I will get what I want)
B: By (deadline the goal will be achieved)
B: Because (the reason and motivation for the goal)
S: Strategy (how I will achieve the goal)

We call it "Getting DIBBS on your dreams." DIBBS comes from a slang term that we used to use as kids. When my brothers and I were growing up, each of us wanted to sit in the front seat of my father's car when going anywhere. To determine who got their turn, if you wanted to call it a turn, was the person who was the first to call out, "I got DIBBS on the front seat!" The person who was quick enough that day to say the magic words first was the one who sat in the front with dad.

This is what The MindCoach System is designed for you to do — to get in the front seat of the car and drive yourself to your destination. And the only way you can do that is to first get "DIBBS" — to take command of your life by setting and achieving your dreams and goals.

In the next section, we will explore exactly how to create, design, and write your goals by using this goal setting formula. OK, now let's start setting goals...

SETTING THE PERFECT GOALS

"The secret of getting ahead is getting started. The secret of getting started is breaking your complex, overwhelming tasks into small, manageable tasks and then starting on the first one."

- Mark Twain,
Father of American Literature

1. EXERCISE: GETTING "DIBBS" ON YOUR GOALS!

Since you established your dreams and listed the reasons WHY you want them, it is time to make your dreams a reality. The best way to make your dreams into reality is to transform them into clear, measurable goals! In this exercise, you will take your most important dream and create specific goals for it. Every goal will include three main components: what you want, when you want it, and why you want it.

DIBBS - (DREAMS - I WILL - BY - BECAUSE - STRATEGY)

When writing down your goals, we are only looking to clarify the end destination.

In this exercise, you will be designing and setting goals for your life or business. This exercise will lead you through a goals-setting process that will help you clearly lay out what you need to accomplish. Let me explain the process in detail to help you with this very important exercise.

DIBBS

Dream: Everything starts with a dream! My dream was to look better, feel better, and to do more in my life. I am going to give you an example of how I used the goals-setting process. You may want to review the Dreams section.

D**I**BBS

I will: Start the goal with "I will." This is your goal and no one else's goal, so the first word is "I." The verb "will" is the action word that mobilizes the goals to action with intention. This will determine the action you will take to attain your objective.

DI**B**BS

By: Put a date on your goal. Once you create the motivation by creating as many reasons as you can for that goal, then you will set a target date and deadline for when the goal should be reached. As a general rule, short range goals should be set from one week to five months and longer range goals from six months to five years on. For the weight loss goal, I had two deadlines to meet. The first benchmark deadline was to lose one pound per week, and another was to have the twenty-five gone by that twenty-fifth week. Having the benchmark deadlines infused in the goal program gave me a way to easily monitor if I was on track. When I gained a pound or stayed stagnant, I was able to make the appropriate adjustments to my diet and exercise regime to get the results I was looking for as I lost the weight.

DIB**B**S

Because: It is now time to create compelling reasons why you want to tackle this particular goal. Finding alluring reasons for your goals is the key factor to start the process toward your objective, but also to keep you going when things get difficult. The reasons make you break through the tough times. Reason gives you the ability to jump over, go around, slip under, or simply crash through any barriers that are in your way. Think of the old cowboy movies where the cowboy rides his horse through the countryside. All kinds of obstacles are in his way. To reach their destination, the cowboy and his horse must hop over logs, trot through rivers, duck under trees, step through rocky trains and so on.

Back to my weight loss scenario. To lose twenty-five pounds, I needed a complete reason to keep me motivated to lose the weight because losing weight has some pain involved with it. It is uncomfortable to make this type of change. Since I was in a calorie deficit, I was hungry—very hungry most of the time. In my case, I was extremely hungry for about two weeks, and then after that my body got used to the number of calories it was provided. So, the first two weeks I needed a lot of reasons to stay on the dietary program. I also needed compelling reasons to exercise every day—if I wanted to or not. The reasons I created produced an internal motivation to start me on the process and then keep me consistent in my journey to lose the weight. What were the reasons? Well, I wanted to look better, for one. Since I was feeling sluggish most of the time, I wanted to feel better and be able to do more. I wanted to be able to play ball with my children and run around in the yard without getting out of breath in the first minute. I wanted to be physically healthy, drop a clothing size, have more energy, and so on. By conjuring up as many reasons as I could, I was able to think about *why* I was trying to lose twenty-five pounds (one pound per week for twenty-five weeks), especially when I was hungry and wanted the triple layer chocolate brownie cake and did not feel like lifting heavy weights over my head a hundred times. Strong, compelling reasons make the difference in your success and motivation to keep you on track when setting short range and long range goals.

DIBB**S**

Strategy: Strategy and tactics are the keys to successfully reaching your goals. In the next section, we will do a deep dive into how to develop a strategy to successfully accomplish your goals.

For now, let's take a look at a few examples and templates as to how to create a compelling goal that is based on the dreams you want in your life.

Use the following DIBBS template for converting your top three dreams into specific goals:

I will [insert your dream here] by [insert timeline here] because [insert your reason why here].

GOALS

EXAMPLE:

Your Dream: **To run the Boston marathon**

I will **run the Boston marathon**

By **March 2022**

Because: **I want to die without any regrets!**

YOUR Dream: _____

I will: _____

By: _____

Because: _____

Let's move to the next step in The MindCoach System.

Step 4: Strategy

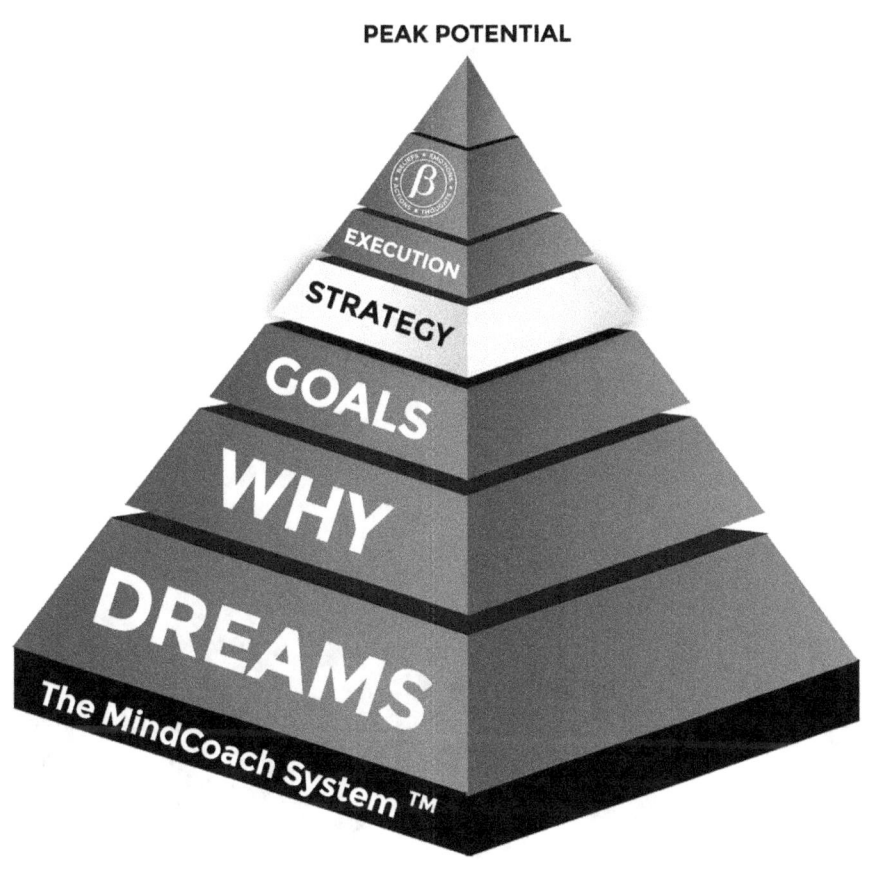

STRATEGY

*What Options Do You Have
And Who Can Help?*

STRATEGY

"Some people say the meek will inherit the earth. I say the strategic will inherit the earth."

- Jay Abraham,
America's Highest Paid Marketing Consultant

How fast do you want to get to where you are going, and what else do you want to build along the way? Many times in life we jump in feet first without taking a long, hard look at the best comprehensive plan of attack. Strategy is all about positioning yourself in the most ethically advantageous way possible, all the while being insanely efficient. Before taking action on your goals, you must first think about the strategy and tactics you will employ to get there. This is the section where you figure out the "how." How will you get to the desired end result? For example, there are hundreds of ways to lose weight, but each one is different. You can choose to follow a paleo diet, vegan diet, do cardio, get a personal trainer, lift weights, cut out sugar, or get your stomach stapled. All can possibly help you lose weight, but which one is right for you? And, which one is in line with your expectations, beliefs, and lifestyle? Before we discuss strategy, you must first understand the difference between tactics and strategy.

- Strategy - defines your long-term goals and how you're planning to achieve them. In other words, your strategy gives you the path you need to follow.
- Tactics - are much more concrete and are the small steps and actions. They may involve best practices, a specific task, resources, etc.

For example, if one of your goals is to create your dream beach body, a tactic may be to lift weights. The strategy, however, would be to create a complete workout plan and routine, including diet. Whether or not you employ the assistance of a personal trainer would also be part of your strategy. Working out with a friend or partner would also add to it. Taking that one step further, you can choose to educate yourself more on best practices in nutrition and weight lifting. As you can see, all these things work together to generate faster results.

To get a consistent result, you need a consistent process to follow. Whether you're baking a cake, changing a tire, creating a computer program, or working through an emotional issue, you will follow a process. Unfortunately, we are not usually provided with a clear mental process for acquiring success and happiness. Throughout our lives, we are inundated with platitudes that tell us to keep our heads up and think on the positive side, but these statements are haphazard at best and not a true "thinking process."

When developing a process for your thinking, you need several components. First, you need a clearly defined problem to solve. Second, you need a filter to cross-reference your ideas with. Third, you need to take a full inventory of your resources. Finally, you need a process to link everything together into a well-formed strategy. All too often, we are taught ways of doing things that are not tied together in a logical, effective, sequential way. When it comes to talking about creating an optimal mindset, it can look very static instead of dynamic and orderly. Once you can learn and adopt a structure for your strategy, and a way to implement it, you are able to replicate it over and over again to produce consistent results.

Ultimately, you will want to employ an effective, proven, successful strategy to reach your goals. Being strategic allows you to think several moves ahead and to be proactive versus being reactive to your situation. Employing a solid strategy will allow you to move faster, farther, and with deeper purpose. Tactics alone are very superficial and do not lead you or others to the next step of the process.

IDENTIFYING A STRATEGY

According to the Harvard Business Review research suggests that 85% of executive leadership teams spend less than one hour per month discussing their strategy with their team, with 50% spending no time at all.

What is strategy? By definition, a strategy is a plan, method, or series of maneuvers for obtaining a specific goal or result. Few people actually write down their goals and even less take the time to think about applying a winning strategy to achieve them. Imagine how much closer to your dreams you can get by layering both of these proven exercises together.

Real thinking takes a lot of hard work; that is why most people tend to simply reorganize what they already know and call it thinking. Human beings love comfort, and it takes a lot of will power and energy to travel into uncomfortable territory. Creative thinking can sometimes be seen as a hindrance, undesirable, and difficult, yet done properly can yield exceptional results. When people begin to think about strategy, they rarely travel far outside of what they already know. They stay within their comfort zone. More times than not the best strategies to implement are ones we are not even aware of. They may exist in a different industry, with another person, in another country, or in a different historical time period. Think about it; how can you find the best strategy to use when you don't know of all the strategies that actually exist? If it does not reside anywhere in your head right now, how the heck can you apply it? This creates a major problem. When choosing a strategy to implement, you must know all the options available in order to effectively choose the best approach to take. Once you take a full inventory of your skills, assets, resources, and relationships you can innovate extraordinary ways to reach your goals. Better yet, you will reach your goals faster, with less effort, and achieve a much higher level than you ever dreamed.

We are all surrounded by simple, obvious solutions that can dramatically increase our results, income, power, influence, and success. The problem is, we just don't see them. A little later in this section I'm going to give you the tools to think outside the four walls of your mind and to also create an efficient filter to quickly sift through everything you come up with.

The time and speed at which you achieve your goals is directly associated with which strategy you choose to utilize. Strategies have the power to both hurt you and help you. All too often people are looking for instant gratification, a quick fix to achieving their goals. Thinking strategically and long-term takes skill and is not for the faint of heart. Developing a strategy can take an exceptional amount of brain power. It can be exhausting, draining, and complicated. Yet until you begin experimenting, you may not know what will actually work. Identifying an effective strategy is often overlooked. People jump right into execution and find themselves working insane hours and staying very busy; however, little progress is being made. Years go by and you find yourself in the same exact spot. I know because I've been there. The scary part was I thought I was really making progress. Every morning my inbox was filled with emails to answer, my computer was exploding with projects to work on and proposals to write, and my phone was ringing off the hook. I was busy with a capital B. I thought I was racing towards my dreams. It wasn't until I faced intense failure that I realized I was not being strategic whatsoever. I did not take the time to connect the dots to my end destination. It was what so many of us call rise and grind. I was grinding all right; I was grinding up my dreams! Until we take a big step back from our daily activities, we don't know what we're doing wrong. It's like the old saying: a fish doesn't know he is swimming in water. We become blinded by what we see every day. This exercise is going to help solve that problem.

STEP 1 - DEFINE THE PROBLEM

There are four parts to building an effective strategy. Number one, you first need to define the problem you are trying to solve. Sometimes it can be difficult to clearly articulate the problem you might be facing. What are you trying to really solve? What is the desired end result? When you formulate your problem, it must be clear and to the point. The more clearly that you define the problem the better results you will generate in the following exercises. I encourage you to recreate your problem in multiple ways using different words and desired outcomes to tease out new solutions. You will be amazed at how just changing one word can completely alter the results of your creative thinking exercises.

Define the problem you are trying to solve:

Example Problem: *I must significantly improve my diet, overall strength, and cardiovascular stamina in order to run the Boston Marathon.*

STEP 2 - CREATE A STRATEGY FILTER

Next you will need to create a filter. The infinite number of possibilities this process will generate can make your head spin. You will need a quick and simple method to sift through the options you identify. It's here you will define what your deal breakers are. You must determine which things are absolutely a must and what are the items that are non-negotiable. These are the things that must be part of your strategy. So, what are the things that you must include in your strategy? For example, if you are allergic to shellfish and your goal is to lose weight, part of your filter must be to exclude shellfish from any weight loss diet you choose. Conversely if you are trying to lose weight and you mandate in your filter that your personal trainer must be good looking with washboard abs and underwear model physique, this may not be a true "must." Identify the key requirements specific to you and that will help you reach your goals. When you create your filter it's important to question what you put down. Sometimes we put things on this list which may not be truly mandatory. You may in fact have some wiggle room to make a certain strategy work if you were pushed to that extreme. You should consider filtering out any strategies that are in direct conflict with such things as your core beliefs, values, health and wellness methods, financial limitations, or your level of risk. You can use this checklist to help mitigate risk, increase happiness, and to save precious time. After you identify strategies to employ you will use the filter to quickly ensure they meet your needs.

EXAMPLE

Your Filter

- ❏ Must be a vegan diet
- ❏ The training must be easy on my knees
- ❏ Must be able to train early in the morning
- ❏ The trainer must have experience training elite runners
- ❏ The trainer must be officially certified and insured

STEP 3 - THE MINDCOACH MATRIX

In step three it's time to get resourceful. Here you will take an inventory of everything you have access to. In most cases when we are aiming to reach our goals there is some form of a lack of resources. If we had the resources whether that be people or money or education, it would not be hard to achieve our goals and we may already have achieved them. More often than not we do not take ample time to think critically about solving this problem. The solution to a lack of resources is the ability to be resourceful instead. Being resourceful takes creative thinking and takes the ability to look at a particular problem differently. You must expand your thinking in order to reach your goals. Believe it or not, you may have untapped resources right under your nose. This could be people you know, skills you have, underutilized relationships or assets or even activities. Maybe you have a regular scheduled night out with friends, or you walk your kids to school daily, or constantly sit in front of a computer. These activities are taken for granted and are rarely thought of as an asset. For example, I walk my kids to school every day. If I am starting a new business, I could place door hangers on the doors of houses on my walk home.

The MindCoach Matrix helps you create an exhaustive list of the skills, assets, people, and resources you have at your disposal. It's designed to overcome tunnel vision and infinitely expand your realm of possibilities. You will be able to cross reference a large number of resources to extract new thoughts, concepts, and possibilities. This is a creative thinking exercise with the intention to carry you outside of your comfort zone. In a way, we are tapping into your mind to uncover hidden gems through the use of simple questions. By pairing two items together, it creates a new search query in your mind. When you see the two items together your mind will automatically begin searching for new associations. The matrix we provided in this book is just a beginning template that you can use. Feel free to add your own elements in order to expand your thinking and generate even more results. Go through the MindCoach Matrix and fill out each intersection. Feel free to revisit this matrix as often as needed when you have new goals to accomplish or challenges to solve. You can download the MindCoach Matrix at www.mindcoachsystem.com. It can also be found in the MindCoach Workbook at the end of the book.

THE MINDCOACH SYSTEM

	You	Family	Friends	People	Professionals	Companies	Educational Institutions	Government	Environmt
Assets									
Products									
Services									
Barter									
Skills									
Technology									
Relationships									
Collaborations									
Distribution									
Opportunities									
Activities									
Events									
Systems									
Acquisitions									

STEP 4 - CREATE A WINNING COMBINATION

You've created a list of your resources and have expanded your options. It's now time to create a winning combination. Once you have completed the MindCoach Matrix you will have all the pieces of the puzzle to build a winning strategy. All you have to do is line them up in an order that expedites your success. How you do this is completely up to you. There are an infinite number of paths to reaching your dreams. The path you choose must be specific to you. Remember, you are your own best coach because no one knows yourself better than you.

It's not just a coincidence that the most notable leaders in every field are master strategists. In the world of martial arts, grandmasters have the superhuman ability to think many moves ahead. When sparring with an opponent, the first series of moves may be to set up or bait their enemy into a position of their choosing. They have the rare ability to not only maximize their own strengths but also to exploit the weaknesses of their enemies. Grandmasters are not only proficient in their respective art, but they also know all the moves they can successfully execute. Moreover, they know what moves their enemy can execute as well. Are you noticing a pattern here? They know what everyone has and then they place them in a calculated order to reach their goal.

INITIAL ACTION

The first move in your case — this may be a phone call, an email, an introduction, or a simple task that starts you on the path to achieving your dreams. Instead of going straight for the kill, think long and hard about your first move. How can you provide value first? How can you give something before you get something in return? Can you get more leverage or credibility somehow by starting in a certain way? In the first column, insert all the tasks or steps that you could do as the initial move.

PRIMARY ACTION

What is your main objective? What is the primary task, action, or step you want to have happen? In the second column, you will list all the items that you foresee being your main move. This may be landing a job, selling a product or service, or securing key relationships. Fill in this column with your primary action.

FINAL ACTION

The third column is your final action. What are the last steps in your winning combination? What things could be done that would solidify your path to achieve your dreams? How can you make it last for longer? Who else would benefit from you pulling off your final move? Your final moves are the ones that if done correctly will make your dreams come true. What are these moves for you? Enter these in the last column.

Finally, connect the dots. Start with the initial action, connect that with the primary action, and lead into your final action. You will have numerous combinations that you can create. Stay flexible in your approach because life always has its way of throwing you curveballs. It's up to you to mix and match them as you see fit to solve your problem and to create a winning strategy.

STRATEGY

EXAMPLE:

Initial Action	Primary Action	Final Action
• Research personal trainers • Hire a nutritionist • Speak with my friend Mark who ran the Boston Marathon • Contact Samantha to be my training partner	• Complete weekly training plan • Record nutrition • Track improvements and progress in running journal • Schedule bi-weekly massage	• Run Boston Marathon • Maintain nutritional changes • Celebrate your success! • Buy Samantha a gift • Continue off-season training

It's time to get to work! We now enter the execution stage of The MindCoach System.

Step 5: Execution

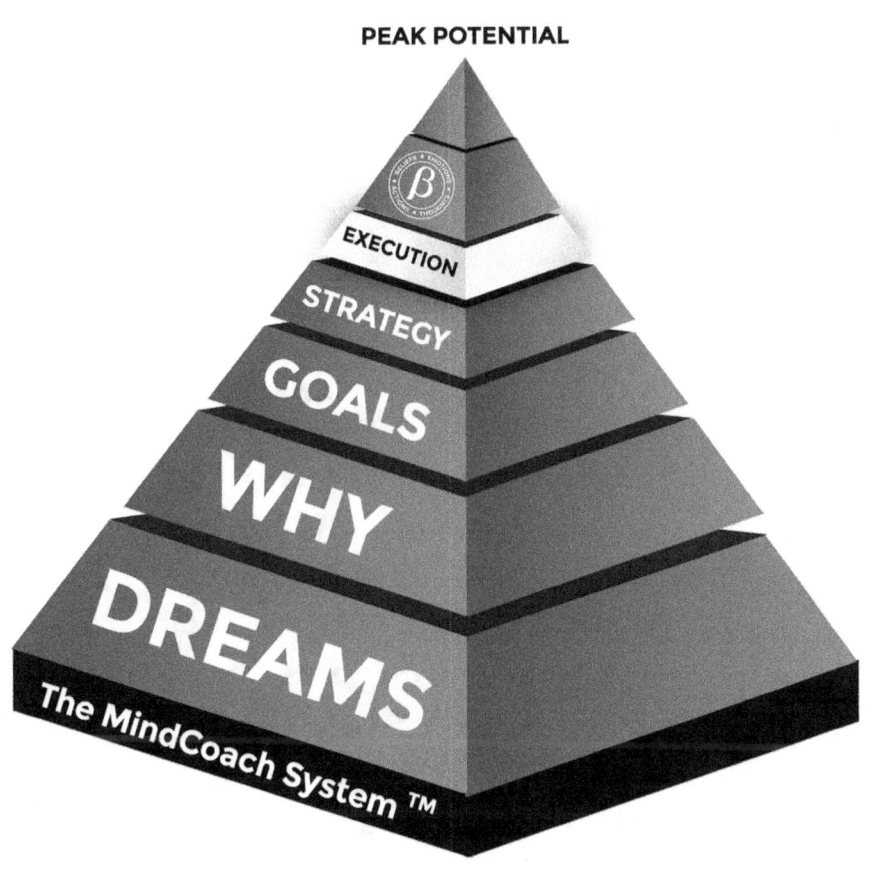

EXECUTION

Take Immediate Action And Develop New Habits

EXECUTION

"We are what we repeatedly do."

- Aristotle,
Greek Philosopher

Taking action is where the "rubber hits the road." This is where you take all the components and begin building your dream life brick by brick. Without action, nothing happens. You can wish, dream, and pray all day every day, but that won't change the digits in your bank account, improve your health, or help you to leave the legacy that you desire. We must act. We must start the physical labor to build the team, meet the people, or complete the tasks necessary to construct our vision into reality. It goes without saying that the more "correct" action you take, the further you travel. Especially in today's world of overwhelming distractions, it becomes easy to get off track. All of us struggle in our own way to stay on track in life. At baseline we all have a level of willpower that can force us to push through undesirable tasks. As much as we may want to deny it, everyone's baseline of will power is different. One's ability to push through, stay focused, and accomplish necessary actions is derived partly through heredity and partly through a lifetime of the experiences they have witnessed and internalized. We would be living in a mystical land of lollipops, unicorns, and rainbows to think everyone is the same in this category. We are all widely different in shape, size, and mindset.

It pisses me off to no end when people flippantly say, "If I can do it, you can too!" The person saying this seems to have no empathy or insight into the current mental barriers or environmental factors the person they are talking to currently faces. Although the message may be said with the best intentions, it is completely ignorant to say something like this without first fully understanding and addressing the differences in both that person's external environment and the internal battle they have in their head. Do not misconstrue what I am saying...it IS likely possible that one can achieve similar results, BUT one must FIRST overcome their own internal and external demons to get there. Without first identifying a strong reason, setting goals, identifying a process, plus challenging and repairing your negative mindset patterns, the action you take will not last. Your willpower will fizzle out and your unconscious will take over again, steering you towards the more familiar comfort, pleasure, and distractions. The person who says, "If I can do it, you can too" is assuming, in essence, "you are exactly like me in every way," and we all know this not to be true. Whether consciously or not, this person has probably already developed a strong "why" and has developed the ability to overcome their inner voice.

EXECUTING YOUR PLAN

At this stage in your life, I assume you already have a system you use for your to-do list. If not, there are hundreds of them out there to choose from and implement. All of them in their own right are excellent. I've been through many of these programs myself. Parts of them I liked, yet parts of them I did not like. I've built my own unique mixed method, borrowing from the different systems to create one that works for me and my style of getting things done. Whatever system you use right now may be just fine, and as long as it works for you that's fantastic.

I learned that the one thing all these organizational and

efficiency systems had in common is that they did not help you to form any type of strategy and did not provide you with any techniques to overcome mindset when you run into a barrier or setback. However, we do want to bring to the forefront of your mind that you must keep your dreams in focus. It becomes overwhelmingly easy to lose sight of our dreams, our goals, and do the things that we must do to enrich ourselves, which ultimately enriches everyone around us. We get caught up in our job, our social media, or the plethora of other distractions that bombard us on a daily, weekly, and monthly basis. The MindCoach System concept is simple; pick two things to do each day that move you closer to achieving your goals. How you incorporate these two tasks into the systems that you already use is completely up to you. We want to make sure you don't lose sight of your dreams. You must continuously make progress towards them.

How do people climb Mount Everest? The answer is simple, one step at a time. Calculated and focused steps one after the other will ultimately get you to your destination. Of course, we all have tasks that arise in our daily lives that we must do that do not relate to our goals, but you need to determine whether these tasks are mandatory or just a distraction. If you find yourself spending time on tasks that are unrelated to your goals or dreams, think twice. There may be ways to delegate, automate, or completely disregard these tasks altogether. You must prioritize the actions you take. Find the ones that will make the biggest difference first and bring them to the front of the line to get done. Here are a few questions to help you prioritize your actions:

1. What is the number one thing you MUST do for yourself or your business in the next twelve months to get you much closer to your goal(s)?

2. What are the top three tasks you MUST do NOW that will move you closer to your goals?
3. What tasks would you consider to be the low-hanging fruit? Which ones are more likely to be successful, profitable, and easier to execute?

Helpful Tips: *When writing your task(s) use an action word or phrase, for example "write email," "call John," "order product,, "verify product,, "thank Stacy," etc.*

Example Daily Tasks:

1. Contact John, my personal trainer, and schedule an appointment to review my goal to run the Boston Marathon.
2. Throw away my large stash of delicious candy I hid in the kitchen cabinet above the oven. Begin cutting out sugar from my diet today. Eat more vegetables.

HABITS AND ROUTINES

Your success depends on the habits and routines you employ on a daily basis. Having dreams, knowing why you want them, setting goals, and having a strategy makes up the foundation of whether you are successful or not. Once your foundation is set, you can execute your plan. However, all too often this plan is not executed routinely. Once you fall off track, you find yourself meandering slowly away from your objectives. Over time, you find that you are off course, or even derailed from your plan. Time passes and you find yourself saying, "What happened? I worked so hard at putting together the components of my success plan, and I failed once again."

Why did you fail? You desperately start to think out loud, "The plan I created was perfect. Everything was clearly stated. I had compelling reasons for my dreams and goals. My goals were clear and measurable. The strategy I worked long and hard on was solid in design. Why did I fail?"

Well, you might have had the best plan, but not being able to execute it consistently turns out to be the ultimate reason you did not succeed. The combination of great planning and consistent execution turns losers into winners almost overnight. Let's think about the greats from history. From Edison and Einstein to Michael Jackson and Michael Jordan, they all had clear dreams and audacious goals. The other important thing that they all had in common was their consistent effort and the habit of hard work and dogged determination to be great. They all had great dreams, but that was not enough. Most importantly, it was sound daily habits and routines that shaped their behaviors to achieve legendary results. Each day, Edison routinely worked on creating the light bulb, Einstein on relativity, Michael Jackson on writing music, and Michael Jordan on his layup shot. Each one of these greats had certain habits that kept them on track to greatness. What habits do you have that are keeping you at your peak potential? What habits do you need to develop?

We all have habits and routines. Most of our habits are unconscious and our routines are, in part, dictated by others. So, the question becomes, "what habits and routines are tied to achieving your dreams?"

Before you answer that question, let's explore the habits and routines you have now. Go through your day and think about each and every action you take, and see which ones are ingrained as a habit in your routine.

- What is your morning routine?
- What things do you do when you get ready for work?
- How much TV do you watch each evening?
- How much time do you spend on the internet?
- Do you set aside time every day to read?
- What do you do for rest and relaxation?
- Do you set time aside to think and strategize your life?
- How do you get ready for work?
- When you start your workday, what is the first thing you do?
- What is your daily exercise routine?

And so on...

Usually, these habits develop incrementally over time. You don't start just doing ten to fifteen habits at once.

Building a habit is like whittling wood. I can remember when I was ten years old. I would scrape my pocket knife down the center of the piece of wood in an attempt to hollow out the center. At first, the wood was flat. As I took my knife over the center surface, it would start to create an indentation in the middle. The more times I cut into the center, the deeper the indentation. This is much like how habits and routines are whittled into your behavior. You first do something several times and your brain begins to make the proverbial indentation into a habit. At this point, the behavior becomes habitual. This is what scientists call *muscle memory*, where less and less thinking is needed to perform the task.

Here is where the problem arises. If these habits are not in line with achieving your dreams, they will not only stymie your progress toward it but will also steal time from the actions and activities you need to be doing to achieve the success you're striving for. So, consciously developing habit patterns and specific routines into your day and matching them with the dreams you desire is essential for success.

Let's take weight loss, for example. Many of us want to lose a pound or two. But, let's say you wanted to lose twenty pounds and get physically fit. Your dream is to look and feel great. You have many reasons to do this, right?. Summer is around the corner, you are going to the beach with your family, you want to look buff on the beach and be ready for that beach volleyball game the guys and girls play every year, and this year you want to finally win a game! You need the energy, vitality, and athleticism to make this happen, and weight loss and becoming physically fit is the way to do it. So, you set your goal to lose 20 pounds. The bathroom scale says you are an even 200. The doctor says 180 pounds would be a good body weight for you. So, you do a little math and figure to weigh 180 pounds it should take you 20 weeks to do this in. You tell yourself, no problem, "I got 20 weeks to lose 20 pounds, which is only 1 pound a week. Piece of cake! Well, not that I will be eating cake in the next 12 weeks," you say to yourself.

You start off great. Excitedly, you look at your kitchen. However, all the food you have is not conducive to losing twenty pounds of body mass. Remember the cake. Yes, it is in the refrigerator, just waiting for you. And yes, it would be a waste to throw it away, wouldn't it? But your plan is solid. You have your eating plan listed out, your calorie counter is ready for the data, your exercise program was designed by your friend who is a certified personal trainer, and you are excited about being buff. Unfortunately, your current dietary habits are sub-par, and your past exercise program was nonexistent. This means you need to flip your behavior patterns totally around. You figure you can jump right into your new lifestyle of healthy eating and vigorous exercise, but you have one major problem. You don't have the habits that give you the consistent actions needed to make this life change. And this is where you stumble. The cake is now in your stomach.

Remember I mentioned you have all the dreams, reasons, goals, and strategies perfectly set up, but they are not executed on the consistent basis to make the plan work. Well, how do you make a new habit? How do you establish a new routine? Most of the time, making a large jump like no exercise to vigorous exercise and eating a lot to eating a little is very challenging and painful. If you did not exercise before and you go out and try to run ten miles, you are most likely going to hurt yourself. Your body is not adjusted to that amount of stress. You need to work into it. This is exactly how you start to develop habits that are commensurate with your dreams and goals.

Start first with one habit and start to change it. Use small increments of change. This will ensure you become acclimated to the new behavior pattern. Then, increase as you begin to adjust to the stress or routine. Remember the story I told you about when I was a boy whittling the wood. I did not take my knife and drive it into the wood one time and carve out the middle. If I tried that, I might have put a gash in my hand instead by slipping and cutting myself. No, I slowly and carefully cut into the wood many times to carve out the center. If you are going to develop a habit, you need to do it carefully, deliberately, and incrementally. Make the changes that are consistent with your plan. This is how new habits are made.

The best way to do this is to replace a bad habit with good habit. By replacing unfavorable habits with favorable ones, you will focus on the habits you want to cement into your daily life. By taking away the old habits like eating cake at night in front of the television, you can replace the cake with carrots or replace nightly television with walking. Still, you want to replace one thing at a time to ensure you bring on new habits and routines into your life.

DEVELOPING NEW HABITS

Along the top of the sheet is where you will write in the new desired habits you want to cultivate. Place a checkmark in the box of the habits you accomplished for each day of the month you successfully executed that habit. Aim to get a minimum of three habits for each day. Keep this worksheet somewhere where you will see it each night. Update this sheet with your accomplishments for the day. Print off a new sheet for each month. A full version of this habit building sheet can be found in the MindCoach Workbook or can be downloaded at www.mindcoachsystem.com.

Now when developing new habits, it is a good idea to have a balance of habits in your daily, weekly, or monthly routine. The MindCoach System provides five categories you can use to start but you can always interchange other categories if you need to.

The five major categories you can use to start forming your habits are the following:

1. Relationships
2. Health and fitness
3. Creativity
4. Build knowledge
5. Evolve mindset

Example:

	Habit 1 Relationships	Habit 2 Health & Fitness	Habit 3 Creativity	Habit 4 Build Knowledge	Habit 5 Evolve Mindset
Month: JANUARY	Time with family	Exercise for 20 minutes	Write in my journal	Read for 30 minutes	Meditate for 5 minutes
1	✓	✓	X	✓	X
2					

REST AND RECOVERY

For centuries, sleep deprivation has been used as an effective military tactic. Keeping the enemy awake for hours on end became a widespread strategy to impair the opposing side's decision-making ability, to get them to break, to gain precious information, or just to wear them down physically, spiritually, and emotionally. Variations of this are used in the controversial application of such things as brainwashing and torture. It's widely known that the human body does require sleep. However, up until recently, we did not understand the true balance between quality rest and a person's productivity. Proper rest and recovery cannot only restore and heal the body, but it can also make you more productive. Resting your body can give you the energy to go harder, longer, faster due to the biological and neurological benefits that result from certain relaxation techniques.

In today's fast paced culture, it has become virtuous to rise early, grind the day out, stay late, and make massive sacrifices to your lifestyle to turn your dreams into reality. You may hear peers say such things as, "wow, they are such a hard worker, I wish I had their drive, where do they get their motivation?" Although their display of a supernatural work ethic is revered by modern society, they may be unknowingly simultaneously sabotaging their overall health, stunting their productivity, and shortening their lifespan. Sleep deprivation has been linked to detrimental issues such as memory issues, trouble with creativity, concentration, mood swings, anxiety, depression, accidents, a weakened immune system, high blood pressure, type 2 diabetes, weight gain, low sex drive, risk of heart disease, and poor balance and coordination. All of which are not good when trying to reach your peak potential.

Research suggests, however. that you may be able to get just as much done, if not more, in a day by scheduling proper rest and relaxation into your routine. Research also suggests that proper rest and recovery has a direct impact on your creativity. Creative tasks such as problem-solving, deductive reasoning, visualization, and physiological performance improve with the right rest and relaxation. Other findings have discovered that mindfulness exercises in the form of meditation have restorative qualities that replenish the brain. Proper rest and recovery restore the chemicals in your brain called neurotransmitters, also known as serotonin and dopamine. It just so happens that serotonin is the chemical our brain produces that makes us feel happy. Serotonin also plays a major role in determining your mood, ability to learn, appetite regulation, and sleep. Dopamine, however, is the foundation of how we feel pleasure. Among other things, it also plays a large part in motivation, how we learn, and how we plan.

Constant stress and anxiety produce cortisol, depleting serotonin and dopamine levels. It actually damages the receptor sites of these neurotransmitters.

Cortisol is the major player in this game of chronic stress. It's responsible for weight gain, particularly increased abdominal fat, and it's been implicated as the leading cause of osteoporosis, digestive problems, hormone imbalances, cancer, heart disease, and diabetes. And, if that weren't enough, it's also responsible for adrenal fatigue, where you are physically exhausted but wired and unable to rest. Adrenal burnout affects your moods, elicits poor sleep, and makes it difficult to concentrate or remember things. That's just the start of the cocktail of dysfunction and damage that cortisol is capable of wrecking on your system.

Chronic stress has been proven to increase inflammation in the brain, enlarging the size of the amygdala, which is for the most part responsible for our emotions. The larger the amygdala gets, the more intense your fear and anxiety becomes. It's a vicious cycle.

Imagine, for example, that you went to the gym and you decided to really go hard. You went three times in one day and pushed your body to the limit through cardio exercises, weight training, and agility drills. It's safe to say that you were going to require a considerable amount of rest and recovery after such a workout. The same principle applies to life. When you push yourself hard during the day, making decisions, communicating, and problem-solving, it takes a toll on your mind. Allowing for an ample amount of recharging allows you to repeat that same effort again. To maximize your performance, you must balance your level of execution with carefully structured and scheduled rest and recovery sessions. Below we have supplied a multitude of ways you can accomplish this. Feel free to take one or more of these and apply them to your daily habits. You will be amazed at how much more you can get done and how much better you feel after you make this a part of your daily regimen.

A study from Carnegie Mellon University (2016) in the journal Biological Psychiatry demystifies the neurobiological effects of cultivating a focused awareness on the present moment.

We've heard it before, but meditation reduces the stress levels in our brain. A study from Carnegie Mellon University published in the Biological Psychiatry Journal has shown that meditation reduces inflammation. Dr. David Creswell, a professor of psychology at the university and the study's lead author, says, "Many people are skeptical about whether there are helpful aspects of mindfulness meditation practices." He continues, "This new work sheds light into what mindfulness training is doing to the brain to produce these inflammatory health benefits."

Mindfulness meditation trains us to ignore the daily traffic of thoughts running through our minds. It teaches us to be still, to be calm, to sit in the present without the fear of the future or the regret of the past impinging on the peace of the moment. Essentially, it does the opposite of stimulating your flight or fight response. It elicits peace and tranquility, producing, if you will, a balance to the stressful stimuli, returning homeostasis to the body.

The blood samples showed that participants who underwent the mindfulness training had lower levels of interleukin-6, a biomarker of inflammation, than those who did the relaxation retreat: "Mindfulness meditation teaches participants how to be more open and attentive to their experiences, even difficult ones," Creswell said. "By contrast, relaxation approaches are good for making the body feel relaxed, but ... [they're] harder to translate when you are dealing with difficult stressors in your daily life."

Scheduling time for rest and recovery will not only help you to be less stressed but will also make you more productive throughout your day. When filling out your habits, add one or more of the rest and recovery techniques below to your day. Here is a short list of rest and recovery techniques to choose from:

Which rest and recovery technique will you implement?	
❏ Meditation ❏ Positive affirmations ❏ Guided visualization ❏ Journaling ❏ Calming arts and crafts projects ❏ Diaphragmatic breathing techniques ❏ Mindful eating	❏ Mindful movement (Yoga, Qigong, Tai Chi, Silat Tuo, etc.) ❏ Mindful exercise ❏ Mindful bodywork (massage, acupuncture, trigger point therapy, etc.) ❏ Taking a mental break ❏ Spend time outside in nature ❏ New experiences

A good and productive life has a balance between hard work and recovery. Working hard on your dreams and striving for your goals can be tasking. Just as someone who uses strength training as a way to build muscle, they are actually tearing down the muscle and creating minor damage to the tissue. After the workout, the body compensates and has a healing mechanism; the body responds to the damaged muscle and builds it back stronger and adds more muscle fibers to compensate for the previous damage. This is done when the body and muscles are at rest, giving the body time to recover stronger than before. There is no difference between you working hard, setting goals, developing strategies, and executing your success plan. Rest and recovery, both mental and physical, is essential for your mind and body to recover so you can come back stronger. Every time you work through The MindCoach System you will need time to rest and recover, only to feel stronger, more confident, and more successful! So, don't forget while scheduling your work — also schedule for rest and recovery. A healthy mind and body need both to be at its peak potential! Congratulations!

There is one last barrier stopping you from reaching your full potential that you need to master. You must have the ability to coach your own mind. It's time for the last and final step, the B.E.T.A. Cycle.

Step 6: The B.E.T.A. Cycle

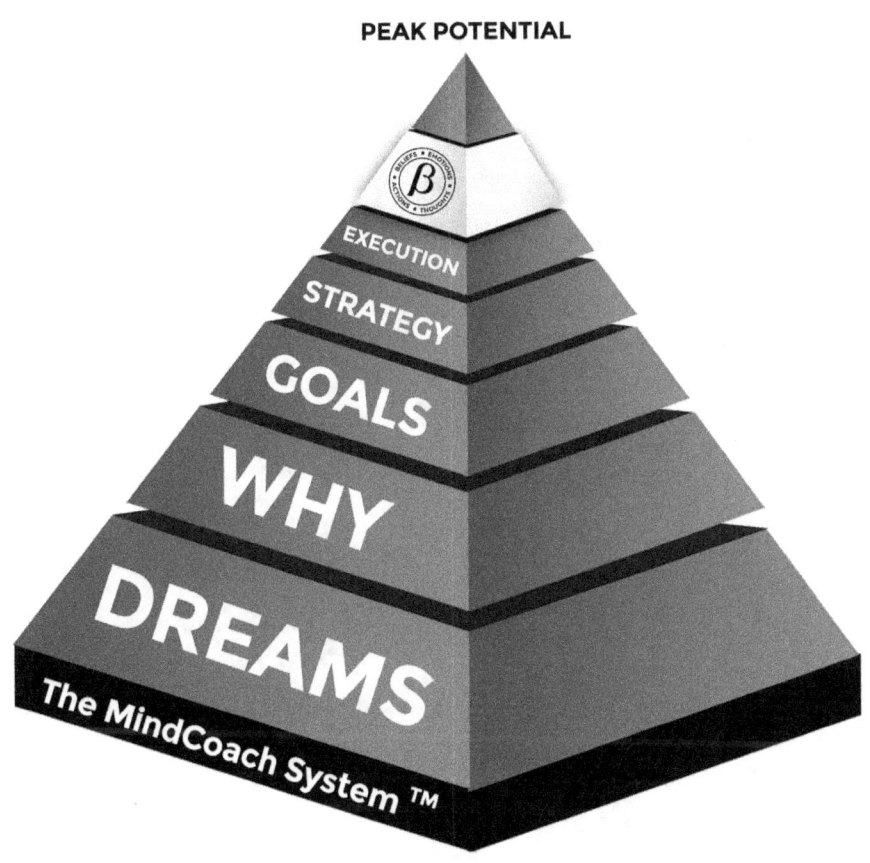

B.E.T.A. CYCLE

What Are You Saying To Yourself?

THE B.E.T.A. CYCLE

"I am not what happened to me, I am what I choose to become."

- Carl Jung,
Founder of Analytical Psychology

The main thing that stops us from reaching our peak potential in life is our own mind. We have the illusion of being in control, but the fact is most of our mind's work goes unchecked. One of the most influential neurologists and the founder of psychoanalysis, Sigmund Freud, often used the metaphor of an iceberg to describe the two major aspects of human personality relating to the conscious and unconscious mind. The tip of the iceberg that extends slightly above the water represents the conscious mind. Beneath the water lies the much larger component of the iceberg, which represents the unconscious mind. It was Freud's belief that sometimes information from the unconscious mind would surface in unexpected ways, like in dreams or in accidental slips of the tongue, also known as Freudian Slips.

If you ever spouted a word or a phrase you did not mean to say, this slip of the tongue response may be due to the unconscious mind controlling the center of your mind at that moment. However, the control center of your mind can be much more of a conscious state of being. The problem is that you don't know ways to take control of it. The components that make up your conscious command center are not well defined and cannot be altered until you know the levers to pull and buttons to push so you can direct your mind in the right way. Not understanding what actually controls your mental acuity and how to consciously change it, manipulate it, and command it leaves you at the mercy of your unconscious thoughts. These unconscious thoughts are relics of your past. Subsequently, you will be enslaved by your past experiences, leaving you responding to your environment, ultimately limiting your decision-making power. Letting your unconscious mind control your behaviors is like driving your car without your hands on the steering wheel. It will not take long until your car drifts off the road and you find yourself upside down in a ditch. That is exactly what happens to you when you don't know how to take control and steer your psyche to stay on the road to success. Taking command of your life is essential as you grip the mental steering wheel and consciously make the necessary decisions as you turn, weave, stop, go, slow down, or speed up. When you experience certain Beliefs, Emotions, Thoughts, or Actions (B.E.T.A.) that are taking you in the wrong direction in life, you are not in control. Learning to steer your mind will help you stay on track. As you drive down the road of life, there will be bumps in the road, stretches of road where you will need to negotiate construction or take unexpected detours that will take you farther than you expected. But all these bumps in the road are a natural progression to the parade of life. It is how you deal with it and (most certainly) how you think of these obstacles that cause distress and heartache. Think about a time where you were in a difficult situation. How did you respond to this in the past? Did you let it control you, or did you have a way to snap out of it? I'm sure at times, like I certainly experienced, you were able to change and control the way you were feeling about that difficult situation, but other times you found yourself in despair, not knowing how to snap out of the negativity of that moment.

So, what is the factor that you need to take control of to become the driving force in your life? First, the conscious state that controls your life is solidly based on scientific evidence. Your brain transitions through different types of brainwaves throughout the day. The one brainwave state that is associated with normal waking state, alertness, logical and critical reasoning, attentiveness, focus, and problem solving and decision making is known as the beta wave state. The beta wave state functions throughout your day, and if left unchecked, can lead to stress, anxiety, and overthinking. However, when this level of brain wave activity is present, you are alert, attentive, focused, and engaged and are more apt to effectively solve problems and make cogent decisions. The positive side of being in a beta wave state is that it also provides the opportunity to control and mitigate any stress or anxiety and stop overthinking, giving you much more control over your mind, emotions, and your body. Too often, however, we allow our beta wave conscious state of mind to run on auto-pilot. In order to make the best decisions, reduce stress, achieve more, and reach your full potential, you must keep your hands on the controls because one thing is for certain, shit does happen, and when it does, you need to be ready to take corrective action.

TAKE BACK CONTROL OF YOUR MIND

So, how and what do you need to take control of your mind's command center? In The MindCoach System, we refer to it as the B.E.T.A. Cycle. Based on what was referred to earlier, B.E.T.A stands for Beliefs, Emotions, Thoughts, and Actions. This is your mind's control center that consciously directs how you think, feel, and behave in each moment. In the following sections in this book, we will detail each one and explain how each one can be used to assist you in taking control, directing, and getting what you want in life.

Whether you want to believe it or not, you have a myriad of Beliefs, Emotions, Thoughts, and Actions (behaviors or habits) that are happening right now as you are reading this that are holding you back from the things you want. In the following exercises, we will be teasing these thoughts out from your unconscious mind and will be replacing them with new ones that will ultimately change your outcomes. Now let's take a look at each one....

BELIEFS

"A belief is not merely an idea that the mind possesses, it is an idea that possesses the mind."

- Robert Oxton Bolt,
English Playwright and a Two-Time Oscar Winning Screenwriter

Now, for one of the most difficult sections - challenging your beliefs. Your beliefs are a combination of not only the things you believe in but also the values that you adhere to. Your values and beliefs have been molded and defined by your unconscious and conscious mind over the course of your lifetime. Your beliefs are the foundation of your moral compass; they help you to decide right from wrong, what to stand for, what to trust, how to act, and how to treat yourself and others. Deep inside your unconscious mind lies a Gordian knot of values and beliefs that you may not even know exist. Sometimes this is the most difficult piece of the B.E.T.A. Cycle to address. It forces you to explore the truth. It makes you take a look at and potentially challenge your past way of living and your deep-seeded sense of identity.

Let's look at some of the beliefs that can get you into major trouble. One of the most common beliefs is that we are "not enough." Somehow, we see ourselves as insufficient, lacking in some way, and we do everything in our power to build up supporting evidence in our heads to support this claim. In addition, some people may think that they do not have enough time, enough money, enough knowledge to do what they need to do in life. Another common belief is that we've already done everything we can; we've tried it all, and nothing works. There are rare cases where these can be true, but even in those situations we still can make a choice to control our minds. Left to its own devices, your mind will conjure up the most devastating beliefs, paralyzing your efforts and negating any and all progress you have made. Its intention is good. It wants to keep you safe and comfortable, but this is typically an uncontrolled response happening from your unconscious mind.

The first thing to realize when addressing your beliefs is to acknowledge that your beliefs are not YOU. Your beliefs were not there as an infant. Even the values that you hold most dear may have changed over your lifetime. Therefore, these are separate and must not be confused with who YOU are. Having the understanding that your beliefs CAN in fact change is one of the first steps. Now, whether or not you actually take the necessary action to identify and replace your beliefs with better ones is another matter altogether. But the truth is you do have the power to change them. There is always another way; there is always something you haven't tried; there are an infinite number of possibilities in the world we live in, and if you recognize this truth, you have the ability to alter your beliefs in a manner that will help you achieve the level of success you deserve in life.

ALL of the beliefs and values that we hold dear have consequences. Some consequences are good and some bad, but they create invisible boundaries around what we do. The first step is to identify the beliefs that may be in the way. For example, "I don't have the money, I don't have the time, and I don't have the knowledge" are very common beliefs.

> **EXERCISE: Identify Your Primary Limiting Belief**
>
> What is the primary thing you tell yourself that you BELIEVE is holding you back from achieving your goal(s)?
>
> What is the primary thing you tell yourself that you BELIEVE that empowers your goal(s)?

EMOTIONS

"Your emotions need to be as educated as your intellect."

- Jim Rohn,
American Entrepreneur, Author and Motivational Speaker

Science has discovered that emotions are, in fact, physical experiences. When an emotion is triggered in your mind, it sends a series of impulses all over your body. Physically, each emotion is programmed differently to cause a very specific physiological response. If we pay close attention, we can sense these changes. When I get frustrated, for example, I can feel my jaw and face tense up. I feel a type of pressure in my body and chest. I begin to breathe slightly more forcefully. I can feel anger just below the surface of my skin, ready to lash out if it is further triggered. How about you?

Numerous scientific studies have found that quantitative changes in motor behavior (for example, increased intensity and duration of muscular action such as during exercise) produce changes in your nervous system (for example, increased heart rate) and in metabolic processes, which generate a plethora of physiological changes (for example, alterations in the levels of hormones, neurotransmitters, trophic factors, endocannabinoids, immune system function) that can elevate your mood and contribute to the reduction of stress, anxiety, and depression. There is also a considerable amount of evidence that suggests that changes in your motor behavior, such as specific facial expressions, postures, and whole-body movements, can enhance these corresponding effects. Since our body is always in some type of a posture, we are unconsciously affecting our mental state.

Several behavior therapy strategies understand this and ask patients to artificially smile, dance, and adjust posture in a way to alter their mood.

We talked about your self-talk and how it generates feelings. The feelings and emotions you experience provide energy to your actions and conduct. These emotions are the engine to the decisions you make, and ultimately are the product of your success. Having control of your emotional state is the factor that will make you or break you. Learning to control your thoughts and being able to recognize how you are feeling is critical to living a fulfilled life.

ANGER: FRIEND OR FOE?

There are many emotions we can analyze. However, there is one in particular that must be mastered - anger. There is a complex series of potentially poisonous physiological events that occur as a person becomes angry. When a person becomes angry, the adrenal glands fill the body with stress hormones, such as adrenaline and cortisol. Your brain diverts blood away from the gut and into your muscles, to prepare you for physical exertion. In addition, your heart rate, blood pressure, body temperature, and respiration increase. Your skin begins to perspire, and your mind becomes fixated on the source of the anger.

Here are just a few of the physical symptoms a person may experience when angry:

- Increased heart rate
- Escalated breathing rate
- Tensing of muscles, especially in the face and neck
- Veins bulge due to increased blood pressure
- Teeth grinding

- Changed facial coloring – most commonly the face turns red but can become pale
- Perspiration
- Body temperature changes - a feeling of hot or cold
- Shaking hands
- Feeling a rush of power (due to the release of adrenaline)
- Narrowed focus

Once you are in an angry state, it becomes virtually impossible to escape its evil clutches. The rush of adrenaline into the body creates an arousal that can last for hours, and sometimes days. It takes a long time for the feeling to dissipate, and during this time most people are still very sensitive and vulnerable to other things that may trigger more anger. If a person is still in this state, seemingly small things can make them snap. Bang, and then the cycle starts over again. Can you see how dangerous this can be if uncontrolled?

Anger more or less starts in the amygdala part of your brain. These two almond shaped structures are responsible for alerting us to potential threats to our well-being. Here is the catch - the amygdala is so fast at warning us about potential threats that it elicits a reaction before we can rationally think or judge the threat (a job done by the cortex part of your brain). In essence, our brain is wired to make us take action before considering the possible consequences of our actions. So, next time someone cuts you off while driving and you decide to express an awe-inspiring display of road rage, and the other driver decides to get out of their car and confront you, just tell them, "I'm sorry for that, my amygdala is not wired to my cortex properly." No, you cannot use this as an excuse for covering up your actions. Managing anger is a learned skill because physiologically you are not born to think first before you act.

According to the research of Jennifer Lerner, a professor of public policy and management at Harvard, emotions, and anger in particular, can have negative effects on decision-making. Whereas fear scares people with a sense of uncertainty, anger can instill a false sense of confidence. Anger makes people more likely to take unnecessary risks and they tend to minimize how potentially dangerous those risks can be.

I've decided to make anger its own section because I realized when I was experiencing tough times much of my struggles morphed into anger. Not only did it make me feel lousy, but it had permanent detrimental effects on my life. My feelings of loss, sadness, and other impulses of self-flagellation ended up externalizing into actions. I would wake up angry, staring at the ceiling and not wanting to get out of bed. My mind would be racing, replaying the triggering event over and over in my head. It would play on repeat in my mind and nothing could stop it. Have you ever felt like this before? I now understand how emotions can lead people to indulge in laziness, social media, alcohol, sex, and drugs to an unhealthy, self-destructive level. People seek out other unproductive distractions just to find a temporary escape from their own head. For me, my anger was unrelenting; I would blindly externalize my anger verbally, and sometimes physically, throughout my day. Sometimes it would unconsciously surface when dealing with other people. I would snap verbally at my children and threaten a punishment much worse than the grievance they committed in the first place. At that moment, my internal anger just added gasoline to the fire. My normally even-keeled persona would transform into a snappy, sarcastic a-hole. My anger would instantly boil up into road rage when another driver did something I felt idiotic. Even the people I was dealing with at work would sometimes feel the wrath of my internal struggles when, in fact, it had nothing to do with them.

Here is the scary part. I was completely unaware that my own thoughts were producing these unconscious behaviors. My actions were negatively affecting the people around me that I care about most. I would go for days not even realizing it was still there. I just felt the anger and frustration but did not go any deeper into my own psyche to unravel what was really happening or better yet to question my mind. To think - how much permanent damage did I really do to my relationships, my family, my children, and my life? That time is gone, and I can never get it back, but I can tell you this - if I were to add it all up, it would equal months, if not years, of being in that state of mind. What could have I accomplished in that same amount of time with the right mindset? What friendships could I have made, what connections with my kids did I miss, and what actions did I not take because I was angry? I will never know the true answer.

Everyone handles stress, anxiety, and fear differently. Some people may become depressed, some may feel sad, some may conjure up elaborate lies just to try and convince themselves of a false truth to make it more bearable to live with their choices. For me, most of the failures I experienced materialized in the form of anger.

Have you ever made the mistake of dropping a soda can in a scalding hot bonfire? Or maybe you've tossed one in there on purpose? (Do not try this at home, by the way). Let's just say this is a metaphor for how I handled failure. Like the can, I sat in the fire and absorbed the heat for a long time. I would internalize all the judgements, anxiety, and stress, and on the outside, everything would look just fine. Eventually, you would witness a small bubble forming on the can, or an uncharacteristic reaction from me. However, when the pressure inside the can reaches a certain point, its integrity becomes compromised. Without warning, the can instantaneously creates a vicious explosion. That small, harmless can turns into a deadly bomb. When it explodes, it does not care about who or what is around it; everything will feel its wrath. After the metaphorical explosion, I would try to pick up all the little pieces of shrapnel, but everything around me had already been destroyed. The damage was done and very little of it could be put back together again. For me, this is how it manifested.

Anger paralyzed my progress in life, and ultimately wasted time I can never get back. Please don't make the same mistake I did. The truth is, I had the power to change it. I always had the innate ability to choose my actions, to reflect on my experiences, and to rethink more effective ways to analyze the situation and dissipate my anger. It all starts with awareness because you cannot change something you are unaware of. Ultimately, you need to substitute alternative beliefs, emotions, thoughts, and actions that you can stand behind. The B.E.T.A. Cycle is a powerful tool whether it's for yourself or used as a tool to analyze others' mindset, it works.

Maybe you are like me and this is how you handle the pressure that you feel each day. There are many other ways that people handle stress, and I encourage you to think about what behaviors come to the surface when you feel angry. Some people have a shorter fuse than others. Some have no fuse whatsoever and stay cool as a cucumber even when the world is burning. So, how do you act? What do you do to escape your feelings? Jot down some quick notes as to how you behaved the last time you were angry. Did you say something or do something that you regret? Do you justify your behavior? What has this behavior cost you in terms of friendships, personal peace of mind, or opportunities?

Every emotion we experience comes with its own inherent

set of pluses and minuses. Whether you're experiencing depression, fear, anxiety, or happiness, contentment, and gratitude, your mind will formulate its own unique beliefs, emotions, thoughts, and actions within each one. It's your job to now become aware of when this is happening and take corrective action before the emotion clouds your judgement.

The MindCoach System utilizes a method called Emotional Self-Talk. This engages not only the verbal aspect but the physical aspect as well. Use this exercise whenever you feel unmotivated, sad, upset, or any form of anxiety creeping in.

IMPORTANT: When practicing this exercise, you must tap into your emotions. Say the words you choose with vigor. Make sure your body is in a powerful posture, ideally standing. Imagine a cape draping off your back like Superman or Superwoman, or like you are standing at the top of Mount Everest. You might look a little crazy when you do it, BUT it works!!! You will be introduced to this exercise later on. For now, it's important to get a basic understanding of the four components that make up your mindset.

THOUGHTS

"All we are is the result of all we have thought."

- Buddha,
Ancient Indian Philosopher and Spiritual Teacher

While self-talk research is ongoing, the Mayo Clinic experts say redirecting negative thoughts toward the positive may lead to: Increased life span, Lower rates of depression, Lower levels of distress, Better psychological and physical well-being, Better cardiovascular health and reduced risk of death from cardiovascular disease. - The Mayo Clinic

When something happens, we immediately give that occurrence a meaning. Our minds work to define what just happened by filtering it through our personal beliefs, values, and past experiences. Many times, if two or more people experience the exact same thing at the same time, they usually have a wide range of thoughts about what just happened.

What are you saying to yourself right now? What feelings are you experiencing right now? You talk to yourself all day long. Do you know that you have about 60,000 thoughts a day? The problem is that you are unaware of the majority of those thoughts that enter and exit your mind. Self-talk is one of the generators to how you feel, and thus, how you respond. Your self-talk (internal dialogue) is connected to your feelings and emotions, and your feelings are connected to your behavior, and your behavior is how you act and respond to your environment. If you want to maximize your performance, you must be in command of what you say to yourself. So, if you are a product of your thoughts, how do you take control of the 60,000 thoughts and make them work for you instead of against you?

Psychological research on self-talk dates back to the 1880s, and across the years much of the research has focused on the fields, courts, and arenas of sports. Well, life is a sport. There are winners and there are losers. And how you think, what you think, and when you think determines if you win or lose. Think about it. Have you ever been alone with your thoughts? How did you feel? Did you feel angry, frustrated, depressed, hopeless, anxious … or happy, elated, joyful? Whatever emotion you were experiencing, you had a certain dialogue running through your head that spawned those feelings. Did you feel like you could take on the world, or did you feel the weight of the world was on your shoulders? It totally depended on what you were unconsciously saying inside your head at the time, if you know it or not. So, the question is, "how do we consistently generate the winning self-talk?" Well, there are techniques and tools that you can implement to produce positive emotional self-talk so you can find the power and potential in yourself. You can set yourself up for success by using positive self-talk, and you alone get to pick the message. You are in complete control of what you say to yourself. If the words of others echo in your head, do not feel compelled to incorporate them into your internal dialog. Ultimately, you choose what you say to yourself, and the associated feelings. This is the power of self-talk.

Many of us have made it a habit of using negative self-talk on a daily basis. This habit can be a bad thing if you employ phrases that cause frustration rather than fervor. If your self-talk is replete with positive statements and motivation, it can help you stay in the present and totally focused on a task. Using such self-talk in a consistent manner will produce positive action and make your actions automatic, consequently heightening your intuition. A sense of mindfulness will become the norm. Things around you will seem more obvious as your internal dialogue becomes more positive. With self-talk, it can be used to motivate you and fill you with the desire to be successful. This is yet another tool that takes you to that next level once you master it.

Many times, the thoughts we have do not support us. They can hinder progress and create detrimental emotions, behaviors, and beliefs within us. The ultimate goal is to convert your negative thought patterns into powerful and truthful statements that will change how you think.

REFRAME THE SITUATION

To change how you think and look at your situation, let me explain an effective mental strategy technique called "Reframing." Reframing is a technique commonly used by counseling psychologists and is an effective way to help others change their perspectives and create more resourceful and advantageous feelings and emotions.

To illustrate the power of reframing, let me give you an example. I was on a connecting flight from Denver to Pittsburgh from a business trip and during the three-hour cross country stint, I ended up, as I usually do, striking up a conversation with a guy who was sitting next to me in seat 12A. During this turbulent flight, I found that John was a successful business owner and was in his fifth year in business. As we talked, he seemed irritated and even angry at times as he explained his business to me.

John said angrily, "Yeah, Uncle Sam and the government keeps taking more and more each year from me! Twenty percent the first year, twenty-six percent the second — and this year alone I paid Uncle Sam over thirty-three percent in taxes. The government takes too much! It is just not fair!"

At this point, I noticed that he was looking at his situation in just one way — a negative way.

I then said, "Well, that is great!

He slid back, cocked his head to the side and said, "What do you mean, 'great'? I keep paying more tax every year. That is terrible and unfair."

I said, 'Well, you are in business, right? And the goal of your business is to grow?"

John replied, "Yes, of course."

I said, "What does it mean when you pay more taxes?

John said, "I made more money."

I said, "Yeah, you are paying more taxes each year because your business is growing by leaps and bounds each year, and you are making a lot more money each year.

John then said, "When you put it that way, that sounds a whole lot better than what I was thinking. When I think about more taxes, I should really think more about how much more money I made. Thank you for that change in perspective. I feel better now. No, actually, I feel pretty darn good!"

Then he said, "I can't wait to pay those taxes!

See, John needed to change his perspective and reframe his thinking. Essentially, the more financially successful John got, the angrier and more jaded he became. With just a little reframe in perspective, John was able to take the same situation, same money, and same business and reframe it to his advantage, not his detriment. This is the power of reframing. Try using this powerful mental tool anytime you find yourself thinking negatively and try to turn it around by reframing the situation or perspective.

ACTIONS

"The 'self-image' is the key to human personality and human behavior. Change the self-image and you change the personality and the behavior."

- Maxwell Maltz,
Author of Psycho-Cybernetics

According to Webster's Dictionary, a behavior is defined as "anything that an organism does involving action and response to stimulation." The fact is, the actions you take or the messages you communicate are external expressions of your unconscious and conscious mind. A portion of behaviors we express are preprogrammed within us by heredity and the remaining are adopted by us after experiencing the ups and downs of life. In either case, we have the power to challenge unwanted behaviors that are not serving us. As mentioned earlier, there are only three factors that elicit a response in our unconscious mind, teasing out both our inherited and programmed behaviors. As a reminder, here are the 3 factors:

ESP (ENVIRONMENT - SELF - PEOPLE)

Environment - *external influences that happen*

Self - *internal representation & perspectives*

People - *other groups or individuals*

Understanding who, where, and what triggers your unwanted behaviors is the key to coaching your mind. You must begin by being able to identify the "trigger" to start repairing your unwanted behaviors. Your behavior is a major factor in shaping your destiny. The actions you take or don't take ultimately define who you are and what you get in life. For these purposes, inaction is a kind of action/decision. Any actions you take will produce a result. And, depending on the circumstances and your decision to take action, you will always move closer or farther away from your goals. Having a tool to become aware of, assess, and take corrective action on your behavior is the key to your success or failure. Doing the right things at the right time in the right way takes skill, experience, and a splash of wisdom.

How we conduct ourselves in certain situations can make or break us. Expressing the wrong behavior or less beneficial behavior at any given time can stir up all kinds of trouble. For example, screaming at your boss, remaining silent when you should speak up, standing in the corner at a family function, displaying a lack of confidence in a business negotiation, acting selfishly (and the list goes on and on) are just a few behaviors that could bite you in the ass if it's not the behavior that gets the best result. The effects of our lack of control over our behaviors leaves our destiny to chance. Otherwise, thoughts, emotions, and beliefs trigger physical responses that just shoot out of our bodies unfiltered and uncontrolled. Many times, it's too late to catch it before it comes out. Imagine squeezing a tube of toothpaste into your hand; now try to put the toothpaste back in. It's a mess to clean up and virtually impossible to put back in. Our behaviors and conduct act in a similar way.

Ready for the good news? You CAN change your behaviors. You can repair these unwanted behaviors to work FOR you, not against you. Why would we ever consider expressing anything less than the optimal behavior for the action we are taking? When you take back control of your behaviors and use them to serve you, life becomes pleasurable again. YOU are now steering the ship, not the environment, not other people, not even your unconscious mind. Now, the way you conduct yourself is deliberate, calculated, and most of all, it gets you to your goals faster. You become proud of your newfound "personality" and others become impressed. Are you ready to get started? Here is a tool you can use to begin repairing your unfavorable behaviors:

You have heard the saying, "Practice makes perfect," right? Well, Mental Rehearsal is a way for us to practice new behaviors without the potential unwanted aftereffects of the real thing. It helps you cope with distractions, anxiety, or negative thinking. Mentally preparing yourself helps you see yourself, hear yourself, and feel yourself respond more effectively to situations that arise. You can mentally rehearse anything you want to do in your life. Each time you think of a situation, you become the actor in that movie scene, doing the action. You are the star of your own life, but with that you are not just the actor. You are the writer, director, producer, and star of your life's movie. Developing the skill of mentally rehearsing is the key to your performance and actions. From the boardroom to the bedroom, once you can see yourself doing your best, performing at your highest, you will reach your full potential.

Mental rehearsal helps you deal with difficult situations before they actually occur. It prepares you for the actions you would need to take in a precarious situation and helps you perform in that situation more aptly than if you were blindsided by it. By practicing mental rehearsal, it is like a buffer to your learning of a real-life situation, and subsequently lacks the real-life consequences that sometimes occur in the real world.

When you think of the attitude and focus you want to transpose into your performance and in your life, you must mentally prepare yourself for what you want to do in a real-life situation. This will enhance performance and eliminate potential problems that can otherwise negatively affect the outcome you desire. Like developing any skill, mental rehearsal takes energy and practice.

THE MIND'S EYE & THE BETA CYCLE

"All problems are illusions of the mind."

- Eckhart Tolle,
Spiritual Teacher and Best-Selling Author

When I was a child, we used to go over to my grandparent's house for dinner every Friday night. I would always look forward to this since I knew it would be an evening filled with laughs, family updates, and (most importantly) delicious homemade food. My grandmother was a phenomenal cook and loved to show off her skills whenever she had guests. As we entered their home, I was overwhelmed with the amazing smell of chocolate chip cookies, brisket, and homemade chicken noodle soup. The house was a time warp back into the '70s with baby blue carpet, a loud floral couch, handmade stained-glass accessories, and disco-inspired wallpaper. The house would be bustling with my massive extended family of aunts, uncles, and cousins. My grandfather was a jokester, taking extreme pleasure in making us laugh hysterically from the most recent joke he learned. He was a large, jovial man with an infectious laugh and a warm, loving demeanor. After giving him a welcome hug and peck on the cheek, I would sit down at the kitchen table with him. While my grandmother was preparing dinner, my grandfather would break out his infamous deck of cards. Smiling, he would hand the deck of cards over to me and ask me to shuffle the deck. I would mix up the cards, restacking and shuffling vigorously over and over again, because I knew what was coming next. I would hand the deck back to my grandfather and then he would set it on the table. Next, he would instruct me to split the deck into four equal stacks. He would then ask me to move the top cards from each stack randomly to the other four stacks. At some arbitrary point in time, he would tell me to stop. He waved his hand dramatically over the top of the cards and then asked me to flip over the top card of each of the four stacks. Slowly, I flipped over the top cards, secretly hoping it wasn't going to work this time. But it did…again….each of the top cards was an ACE! What kind of impossible sorcery was this!!! Either my grandfather had the best memory on the planet, or he was seriously a freaking magician!

Years went by and I could never figure out that damn trick. It baffled me each and every time he performed it. It wasn't until many years later, after incessantly asking for him to divulge the secret, that he shared the trick with me. Before sitting down at the table, he would stack the deck, finding all the aces and placing them on the top of the deck. From there he always knew where they were. Of course, once he told me how it worked, it completely demystified the trick. Thirty-five years later, now with my own kids, I can easily execute this same card trick on them, smiling as I watch the same look of disbelief and amazement on their faces.

Once we demystify how our mind works, it no longer can trick us with illusions. Similar to my grandfather's card trick, our minds can be a mystical abyss where magic happens, where thoughts appear and disappear. The mind can conjure up emotions and all sorts of thoughts, both positive and negative. Many times, it seems like it cannot be tamed, and we are destined to be on the emotional roller coaster ride of a lifetime. Although our thoughts, emotions, and whatever else dwells within the deep recesses of our minds add flavor to this thing we call life, they can also be what keeps us from having or becoming what we so desperately desire. Like magic, the mind does not appear to have any pattern that we can detect. Part of the MindCoach goal is to demystify the way you understand your thoughts, emotions, actions, and beliefs. All these things are connected, and each one influences the other. We are ready to reveal the secrets of the "trick" that can change your life.

Everything we do in our life flows through our mind's eye. Both our actions and our inactions get filtered through it. This is where our identity resides, where our values live, and where our beliefs ring true. Think of it as a gatekeeper, letting ideas and actions flow in and out of your mind. Some things are stopped dead in their tracks because, for some reason, our unconscious doesn't agree with them. Other things pass through the gate without effort because they are in line with who we are. The mind's eye is the place where your dreams go to die. It is a black hole and mystical abyss that will generate beliefs, emotions, thoughts, and actions that will either serve you or hurt you. Many people don't even realize it exists, and in the visual we provide you can see it stopping you from reaching your peak potential. The mind's eye never stops working; it is always moving twenty-four hours a day, seven days a week, and three hundred sixty-five days a year. Just know it is always there and it is now your job to monitor what is going in and out of this vortex of thought. The next step in your journey is to better control what is going in and out of your mind's eye. Your mind belongs to you and you alone. Your mind's eye was put there to serve you. In the times it hurts you, just understand it's not on purpose; it is doing its best to protect you. With your conscious direction, your mind's eye can become a source of immeasurable self-power.

E.S.P.

ENVIRONMENT - SELF - PEOPLE

Are you ready for this?! We are about to make this whole MindCoach System even more simple for you. One of the most important skills you can learn is understanding where your mind is being influenced from. There are only three things that influence your mind. Yes, that's it! Read this section carefully because once you understand where and what is influencing your mind you can then create a plan to eradicate the issue that is the limiting force that is stopping you from reaching your full potential. Take back control of your mind with this simple acronym, E.S.P. - Environment, Self, & People:

1. ENVIRONMENT

The environment is one of three main factors that impact your mind. For example, environmental influences may include such things as weather, food, circumstances, situations, illness, and even an act of God. These influences come from beyond yourself and are a result of larger things at play.

Have you ever gone out to your car and found the tire was flat? How did you feel? What did you think? Were you in a hurry to get somewhere? This is where life is a slap in the face. One minute all is well and before you can pass "go" and collect your two hundred dollars, the garage door no longer opens at the push of a button, your furnace conks out in the midst of a cold spell, the washing machine ceases to spin, and your car dies ... all in the same month. That is the gravity of life. Such misfortune may derail you, but the question is how long do you allow it to keep you mired in your misery? Do you jump up and solve the problem or do you keep that problem running through your mind without solving the problem and moving forward?

The difference between successful people and others, who cannot seem to overcome environmental barriers, is the ability to solve problems. When we identify ourselves as the victims of circumstance, we sometimes dwell on the negative and are held hostage in our own minds. When you deal with the problem directly and do not blame others, feel sorry for yourselves, or use the problem as a way to receive love or attention, you regain the power to take back control of your mind and your life. Successful people do not say, "Oh, this always happens to me. Nothing ever goes right for me. Why does this always happen to me?"

When you engage in negative self-talk, your mind tries to answer the questions rather than work to solve the actual problem. Saying, "Why does this always happen to me?" is a monomaniacal statement that focuses all the energy on you, the person, and not the problem. Successful people take what happens at face value and treat it like a problem to be solved. They treat it as an obstacle to jump over, not a brick wall to run into. Their self-talk is different. Their self-talk goes something like this: "What do I need to do to solve this problem? Who can help me solve this issue? Where do I need to go to solve this problem?" Notice the difference between solution-based self-talk versus languishing as a victim. Successful people see what they can do rather than dwell on what happened. The gravity of life is always going to pull you down, but the more important thing to remember is how you deal with that pull. This will all depend on how you look at the situation and what you interpret it to mean to you.

2. SELF

The second major influence in your mind is YOU. Sometimes we are our own worst enemy. We castigate ourselves to a point that is completely unjustified and unfair. You need to get out of your own way! You are unknowingly blocking the road to your true potential. Some examples of this might be saying such things to yourself like the following:

- "I'm not good enough."
- "I'm not smart enough."
- "I'm a bad mother/father/boss."
- "I'm afraid of what others will think."
- "I'm afraid to fail."
- "I'm a loser and nobody likes me."
- "Nothing good ever happens to me."
- "I don't deserve it."
- "Everyone is out to get me."
- "I'm weak."
- "I'm unworthy."

You pull yourself down by the beliefs you hold and what you say to yourself. These self-imposed limits create a ceiling for your potential. When you place a ceiling on your own potential, you are unlikely to attempt anything more than you are already doing. When you are mired in comfort, there is no pressure to move. Examples of this type of gravitational pull are bad habits and routines that no longer serve a purpose.

If you think about gravity as physicists do, the more mass an object has, the more gravitational pull it has on other objects. Have you ever "pulled yourself down" by thinking that you were not capable, could not complete a certain task or get a promotion, and consequently felt like a real dunce?

Most of you have experienced this at one time or another. This mindset is your own gravitational pull, which holds you back from taking chances and risking failure.

Let me take this analogy further and illustrate the danger of having too much of a gravitational pull that could make recovery impossible. Our friends in the physics department say that stars that are twenty times larger than our sun go through a process at the end of their lives in which they eventually collapse and form black holes. Stars continuously fuse lighter elements into heavier ones during their lifetimes. During the process of fusion, there is a constant inward pull due to gravity and an outward push due to pressure, such that the two balance each other. If a star is massive enough, it will fuse elements into iron. As more energy goes into fusing iron than is produced, this is the end of the line, and the star runs out of fuel. Gravity wins the battle against pressure, causing the core to collapse under its own mass. At this point, the star's outer layers explode in an extremely violent supernova. When such a core is more than two and a half times as massive as the sun, the inward pull of gravity is so immense that the core continues collapsing upon itself, resulting in the formation of a "black hole." When a black hole is created, the gravity is so immense that even light cannot escape, hence the name "black hole."

This analogy has psychic parallels to how we single-handedly destroy our motivation and belief in ourselves. If you play this out and compare a star's collapse due to energy depletion and how we can eventually collapse psychologically, there are stark similarities. Let me provide the parallel.

First, we will examine the star that starts to fuse lighter elements to heavier ones. This is no different from when you have small, irritating problems in your mind, but make them feel larger and heavier than they really are. It is the old adage, "making a mountain out of a molehill," right? Second, there is a constant inward pull due to gravity and outward push due to pressure, such that the two balance each other and pressure starts to build. You build up pressure just as the star does. These feelings become more and more intense, and you find yourself becoming frustrated and angry. At this point, your rational thinking is affected and becomes unclear. Now, in keeping with the supernova example, if the pressure is great enough and the star big enough, then the elements fuse to make iron and the fusion process ends. The star runs out of energy. For you, this is where the pressure within you becomes so great that you shut down and you stop thinking. For the star, gravity wins the battle against the pressure; the core collapses under its own mass and the star's outer layers erupt in a supernova. When the gravity of life takes you to the edge, you implode and explode in some manner. At this point in the life of a star, a black hole forms where light cannot escape. Your black hole is when you feel hopeless and depressed, unmotivated, and unwilling to try. All of this occurs within your mind. The good news is this can be reversed.

3. PEOPLE

Last but not least, there are People. Other people's words, attitudes, and behaviors can have major influences on your mind and, ultimately, your performance in life. Think about the people who care about you. When considering a new endeavor, you may hear whispers and warnings of "You can't do it." Perhaps in an effort to prevent you from failure and the accompanying humiliation, they caringly suggest that "You shouldn't try it." They could also ask, "Why would you want to do that?" Whatever words or phrases they employ, they are telling you, "Why try? You won't succeed at this anyway." Have you ever had this experience? I sure have, on multiple occasions.

These people care about you! They're looking out for your best interests. They do not want you to get hurt or fail. And, since they don't want you to fail (possibly resulting in them feeling bad as well), they tell you not to try. If you do not try, you will not fail, and no one gets hurt! Logical, right? These statements and suggestions are so powerful that it is like having a professional hypnotist around you and providing suggestive statements all day long.

It is disheartening to realize that this attitude pervades the lives of so many. You might say, "Not me. I think for myself. I do not let others dictate my beliefs or drive my dreams." Perhaps if you live alone, buddy up to the television, avoid the workplace, and merely stay at home staring at walls, you can think what you want to think and hypnotize yourself in any way you choose.

Of course, I am not a hypnotist, but even my words are providing suggestions and making you more aware of the influences in your life. You will encounter many people who influence your life in some fashion, for better or worse. If you are hanging out with the wrong people who do not support what you want to do in life, they will attempt to guide you in a negative way. You may not even recognize what they are doing or understand why until it is too late and an opportunity to win the game has passed.

Like viruses, behaviors and attitudes are contagious. If you are around people who are coughing and sneezing, there is a good chance you will pick up the same common cold they have. I guess that is why doctors call it a common cold, because it is so common. When you associate with people who are not aligned with your vision and goals, or worse, surreptitiously influence your mind and behaviors, you may be inclined to start acting like they act, or believing what they believe. You pick up certain patterns of behavior and find yourself spending time in the wrong places at the wrong times.

Nature provides a number of examples of this phenomenon. A case in point is the zombie ant. As it turns out, some ants that live in the rainforest venture from the high tops of the trees at night. In doing so, some encounter a fungus that attaches itself to the ant and burrows into its body. It makes its way to the ant's brain, controls the ant's behavior, and convinces it to stagger away from the ant colony. The ant eventually climbs up a tree, attaches itself to a branch using its pinchers, and dies. After this happens, the fungus uses enzymes to break down the ant's hard exoskeleton and the fungus grows out and up from its head (creepy). This graphic analogy should say something about the nature of those with whom you hang out.

Yikes! Is it really that bad? Are your questionable acquaintances prepared to take over your life with their intrusive thoughts, crowding your head like fungi? I would argue that this is indeed what is happening (minus your head exploding and fungi growing upward from your skull). These people are using any means possible (such as ideologies, persuasions, propaganda, and good old-fashioned goading) to influence you. Now, if that does not feel like fungi saturating your poor brain, I do not know what is. What you watch on television, what you read, the music you listen to, the people you associate with, and virtually anything that infiltrates your consciousness may affect your psyche, thoughts, beliefs, and behaviors, if you let them!

THE 3A's

AWARENESS - ASSESSMENT - ACTION

"You become what you give your attention to."

Epictetus,
The Art of Living: The Classical Manual on Virtue, Happiness and Effectiveness

There are three steps that we must understand before we can effectively make any changes within our minds. The 3 A's (Awareness, Assessment, Action), will help you change your mental and emotional state, resulting in empowering actions. They can push through barriers. As we continue on our journey to become the best versions of ourselves, it's difficult to see what's really stopping us. Half of the battle is discovering what it is, and that it even exists in the first place. Have you ever worn a pair of glasses for so long that you totally forget you are wearing them? Everything outside of you appears normal, but you are still wearing the glasses. Our unconscious mind creates our own personalized filter that influences how we view life in the same way a pair of glasses may work. Some glasses may enhance and enlarge images, others may change the color around us, but until we remove those framed spectacles from our eyes, we will not know what the real world around us looks like. If we recognize we are wearing a pair of glasses, we can remove them and look at what they are made of. We can then decide whether it's the best pair of glasses to be wearing for the situation at hand. By using all 3 A's you will be able to recognize your thought patterns, assess how your thoughts are making you feel, and take action to change the thoughts and emotions so that you can choose and have access to more empowering, positive behavior patterns and choices. Let's take a look at the 3 A's:

1. AWARENESS

Your awareness is the first key to changing your mental state. If you don't know what is happening, you can't change it. Have you ever been "talked into doing something" and then later realized you were manipulated into doing that thing? Well, the reason you did it (for sake of simplicity) is that you were not <u>aware</u> what was happening at the time. This is why you fell for the message that was being sent. This is no different when you are not aware of your own words, phrases, and messages that are rumbling through your head every minute of the day. We have all found ourselves feeling upset, perhaps irritated or angry, but have no idea why or where the feelings came from or why we feel the way we do at that moment.

This happened to me just the other day. It was about midday, and I had a scheduled appointment with a business associate. During our discussion, she asked how I was doing. I thought it was strange she would ask this halfway through the call but, apparently, she had a reason. I was taken aback by the question but did respond by saying,

"You know, I feel a little irritated right now. Not sure why, but I do."

She apparently sensed irritation in my voice. Now, since she brought that to my attention, I was keenly aware of how I was communicating, and I was able to quell any other verbal peccadillos I was sending to her and we finished the call on a positive note.

However, after the call, I started to think about why I was feeling so annoyed. I quickly realized that I was thinking about a previous conference call I had two hours earlier where a deal did not go through. I was upset about the outcome and blamed myself. I realized all the negative statements were *renting space* in my head and I was declaring that I "should have gotten the deal and it was not fair." Moreover, I realized I was saying "I was downright brainless for not negotiating the deal more skillfully." The negative dialogue was living in my head during the next call. As a result, I was not aware I was producing these negative thoughts until my behavior was brought to my attention. Moreover, my ability to process and think about what was really making me feel so irritated gave me a sense of awareness and control I needed to change my thought patterns, my feelings, and my responses. Having the awareness is the first skill in the process of being able to change your mind, emotions, and behaviors.

THE RETICULAR ACTIVATING SYSTEM (RAS)

Awareness begins in our brain, and in recent years neuroscientists have discovered that we have a mechanism that helps with just that. The reticular activating system (RAS) is a section of the brain that begins close to the top of your spinal column and extends up about two inches. It has the diameter of a crayon. All your senses, except smell, flow directly through this bundle of neurons. Although small, it plays a critical role in your awareness. It acts as a gatekeeper, or bouncer, of the information that is let into your conscious mind. The RAS has the responsibility of filtering out all the sensory information that is being thrown at it all day long and selecting the bits that are most important for you to pay attention to. Imagine the amount of information around you going on at all times; it's completely overwhelming. It is estimated that the conscious mind can only handle around 100 pieces of information every second. The RAS has the unique ability to pare this down to the ones that are most important. We can train our RAS to "look for," or pay attention to, the things we want more of in life. This is why the RAS plays an important role in motivation and goal setting.

A good example of this is when I was looking for a new car. Once I began looking for a certain type of automobile, I started to notice more and more of that particular make, model, and year on the road. After about two weeks, I must have noticed over 30 cars that were the same make and model as the one I wanted to buy. Why did this happen? Well, it is due to my reticular activating system. Since I had this certain car in mind, my brain was focused in to notice that particular car, and I was more aware of it when I saw the car. The number of cars on the road did not change; only what I was looking for changed. Before my search for a new automobile, I just was not focused on that type of car. Your awareness is biologically driven, and it is the first part of the equation to taking control of your life and business.

Think about setting goals. How does this actually work? When you set a goal, you focus on one particular thing you want for your future. When you set your goal, you have a visual representation of what you want to achieve, obtain, or be. Your mind is now open to all the things that relate to that goal. You begin to see opportunities you did not see before, which helps you reach that goal. You can thank your reticular activating system for that.

Let's take weight loss. This is a popular goal that people set for themselves. Usually around the beginning of each year, people proclaim to themselves that their goal is to lose twenty pounds. If you do this, what do you start to think about and notice? You start to notice the workout garments that others are wearing, the people running in your neighborhood, diet and fitness books in the bookstore, fitness centers in your town, the food that is in your refrigerator, the food and calorie count on a restaurant's menu, and the list goes on and on. You start to pay attention to aspects that relate to your ultimate goal, and where you focus your awareness brings opportunities for success. Your success is totally determined by what you focus on in your mind's eye. However, let's examine what the next step is after you have become aware of the problem, situation, or goal.

2. ASSESSMENT

The second step in the 3A's process is assessing what and how you are communicating to yourself. Here is a quick assessment to analyze what you are saying to yourself:

> **EXERCISE:**
>
> 1. What generated the thought, feeling or behavior?
>   a. Environment?
>   b. Self?
>   c. People?
> 2. How was your thought, feeling, or behavior triggered? What was the exact trigger?
> 3. Where is this conflict coming from? Which of these is it in conflict with?
>   a. Your core values?
>   b. Your core beliefs?
>   c. The identity you have of yourself?
> 4. When & where did this internal conflict originate from?
>   a. Past history?
>   b. Present?
>   c. Future (i.e., fears, anxiety, excitement, etc.)?

3. ACTION

The actions you take will determine your mental state, thus changing the way you feel. Your ability to change your mental state is an ongoing practice, and it takes repetition and training. This will help you to develop a strategy to follow, making the probability of success much higher than if you did not have one.

Changing your actions changes your physiology and alters a myriad of biological processes such as blood flow, blood pressure, heart rate, breathing patterns, muscle tension or relaxation, and many more. As a result, this provides the resources to think more clearly and be more creative when processing your thoughts. In this section of the exercise, you will list the actions you can take and do to make these physiological processes work for you.

There are four tactics/action steps you can use that will make up your peak performance mental strategy:

1. **REFRAME THE MESSAGE** - Replace or rephrase the mental message you are saying to yourself. Find alternative empowering meanings that serve you instead of hurt you. Use words that help you to gain a higher perspective on the issue.
2. **CHANGE YOUR PHYSIOLOGY** - For example, standing up, sitting down, walking, jumping, running, changing your posture or facial expression, or conducting deep breathing exercises.
3. **CHANGE YOUR LOCATION** - Walk to a different room, go outside, go to your car, distract yourself with something else, like music, TV, or recreation.
4. **CHANGE YOUR HABITS AND ROUTINES** - Waking up earlier, exercising, eating, sleeping, household tasks, work schedule.

AWARENESS	ASSESSMENT	ACTION
• What are you saying to yourself? • How are you feeling? • What is the image you have in your mind?	• What generated the thought, feeling, or behavior? (Environment, Self, or People) • How was your thought, feeling or behavior triggered? What was the exact trigger? • What value, belief, or aspect of your identity is this in conflict with? • When & where did this internal conflict originate from?	• Reframe, replace, repel the mental message. • Change your physiology. • Change your location. • Change your habits or routines.

CREATE SEPARATION

Creating space between you and your **B**eliefs, **E**motions, **T**houghts, and **A**ctions (your **B.E.T.A.**) is a foundational component of taking back control of your mind. The more separation we are able to create, the more subjective, rational, and at peace we can become. When my clients are stuck and are having trouble seeing life in a constructive way, I always tell them that "a fish does not know it is swimming in water." When we find ourselves swimming around in our own heads, we are not able, at that time, to see things in a different way. Remember a time when you had a million things to do, anxiety began mounting, and you became totally overwhelmed and were frozen with fear? And the more you thought about it, the worse it got. In a desperate attempt to get things done, maybe you began to write all the tasks down on a sheet of paper only to find out that you only had seven things to do! It felt like a million things and was totally overwhelming, wasn't it? But, in reality, you only had seven things to do, and only three of those tasks had to be completed that day. Why did writing these tasks down on a sheet of paper make you feel better and more able to get things done? This is the all-important notion of separating your thoughts from your feelings. Just that small amount of space we create has the ability to lighten the burden on our minds, ultimately making us feel better.

Once you are able to see what is in front of you and subjugate the hurricane of thoughts in your head, you are now able to manage your emotions in a much more efficient way. I am not saying you will be instantly happy or at peace, as nice as that would be. What I am saying is that you will be able to take the thoughts and feelings coupled together, bouncing around like a pinball machine, and organize them so that you can make cogent decisions that serve you. Changing our beliefs, emotions, thoughts, and actions using the technique of separation is a road trip, NOT a time machine. Creating separation is used for the sole purpose of identifying a new perspective, gaining clarity, or discovering an alternative point of view.

All the desired feelings we want are already there; they exist. If you are looking for more "happiness," you are not going to find it hiding in the cushions of your couch. All joking aside, the only reason we are not in possession of the feelings we want right now is because our unconscious mind gets in the way. Right now, in this exact moment, you are experiencing beliefs, emotions, thoughts, or actions that are blinding you from living the life you desire. If you first become aware of these hidden monsters, you can bring them out into the light. You can then use the tools and exercises outlined in this system to strip away the mental noises from your identity and replace them with new, more empowering thoughts and actions.

Let's say, for example, you have worked as a janitor for 40 years. You may believe you ARE a janitor, but the truth is that this is something you DO. Your occupation has zero to do with your spirit, your essence, or your identity. Sure, this has heavily influenced your life, but it only defines you if you let it. You may have many important roles in life like being a father, husband, brother, or good friend. Recognizing that you are separate from the things you DO and THINK gives you a newfound freedom to shift your mind.

6 TOOLS FOR MIND COACHING

1. WORDS

The words you use to describe your experiences matter, and matter A LOT. A study conducted by the *Journal of Personality and Social Psychology* found that cueing people to reflect on intense emotional experiences using their names and non-first-person pronouns such as "you" or "he" or "she" consistently helped them to control their thoughts, feelings, and behaviors. This is just a small example of the power that words have on your psyche. And it doesn't stop there.

Answer this question… "Who are you?"

You may say something like this, "My name is Adam, and I was born in Toledo, Ohio. I am 5' 10" and love elevator music and long walks on the beach and so on…." Is there any place on or in your body that has a label saying, "Made in Toledo, Ohio?" Absolutely not. We use words to label who and what we are; ultimately, words shape our identity. Depending on the words we use, this identity can change drastically. For example, saying something like, "I am a smoker," vs., "I was a smoker," or even saying something like, "occasionally I may partake in breathing in a tobacco leaf wrapped in paper," all create very different self-identities, as well as the accompanying mental imagery. If used properly, carefully crafted words can help us to reshape who we think we are. We can create space and separation from undesired beliefs, emotions, thoughts, or actions by weakening the verbiage we use to describe it. The further away from our direct identity we can make it appear, the more powerful of an effect it will have.

2. SYMBOLISM

Some people believe that objects have no inherent meaning, but they are all gravely mistaken. With enough meaning associated with it, a symbol or object can influence your beliefs, alter your emotions, influence your thoughts, and even possess your body. Some symbols have an almost mystical ability to communicate to us without the use of words. It is almost a spiritual experience that transcends comprehension and takes over our senses. Things such as jewelry, clothes, animals, pictures, words, relics, places, music, symbols, and even dance can possess almost magical powers.

Since the origins of humankind and throughout every civilization, objects and symbols have been used to convey meaning. Power objects, talismans, amulets, charms, mascots, and jujus are all names for variations of this same concept. For example, have you ever been to a museum and been so moved by a piece of art that it made you feel something? Have you ever heard a song that brought up long-lost memories? Or have you ever been in the wilderness and seen a large, wild animal up close? How did that make you feel? Perhaps you wear a piece of jewelry from your grandfather that symbolizes the love and happiness he brought to you. Wearing the jewelry may recall vivid memories of him, or just seeing it may remind you of his strength and charm. By incorporating symbols into your daily practice, you can create constant reminders of whatever belief, emotion, thought, or actions you wish to embody. The symbols you wish to use are completely up to you. Depending on where you are in your life journey and what you wish to accomplish, your choice of a symbol or object may be different. The pyramid utilizes powerful words and symbols to trigger one's motivation, commitment, or power. Whether you decide to use our items or find your own doesn't matter, but I highly encourage you to utilize symbols to their fullest extent. Surround yourself with symbols that will help keep you on your path so you can remain focused on achieving your peak potential.

We have all heard the saying that "a picture is worth a thousand words," but in reality, "a symbol is worth a thousand words, thoughts, and emotions." People wear symbols all the time. What do people do with it? Connection with yourself.

The use of a pyramid for The MindCoach System diagram was not by accident. The pyramid is a highly symbolic image. From ancient times to present day, pyramids have been a symbol of power, achievement, and enlightenment. These awe-inspiring structures are considered one of the strongest talismans on planet Earth. They have been a prolific symbol in numerous ancient cultures. A pyramid represents revelation, enlightenment, and a higher perspective. The shape is often used to explain the cycles of growth that lead to a higher state of being. Spiritually, it illustrates a path towards enlightenment or connection to our higher self. The shape itself triangulates energy in the direction of its point. The MindCoach System diagram stands for all these things. By its mere sight, its intention is to instill power, growth, and enlightenment from within you. It will act as your symbolic guide to not only reaching your full potential but also your commitment to creating a better life for yourself. Keep this in plain view, hang it on your wall, and wear it on your body to direct your focus towards where you want to go in life.

If you are interested in applying symbolism to your journey, feel free to visit www.mindcoachsystem.com to view some examples of clothing, posters, or other symbols that can be used as daily reminders.

3. PHYSIOLOGY AND MOVEMENT

Numerous studies have proven that changing your physiology can have an impact on your mood. Simple things like posture, body movement, and facial expressions can have profound effects on our minds.

This isn't just made up voodoo magic; scientific research has confirmed the connection between poor posture and mood, especially in those who are experiencing depression. One study, published by the *Journal of Behavior Therapy and Experimental Psychiatry*, identified that people with mild to moderate depression felt better after simply keeping their back and shoulders upright while sitting. These people also reported a lower level of anxiety.

Another study, published in the journal *Biofeedback*, also had a similar conclusion. Participants who had a slouched posture while walking felt more depressed. When they changed to a more upright position, their energy levels and their mental sharpness increased.

Without going too far into the weeds as to why this happens, many doctors have hypothesized that it has a lot to do with our oxygen consumption, as well as our spinal column. By having correct posture, we optimize the signals to our brain and increase the amount of oxygen simultaneously. This is another reason why exercise is also linked to your mood.

This topic alone can be its own book. For the sake of keeping it simple, you must be cognizant of your physiology. Make sure you're exercising regularly and checking in on yourself to see if you are sitting or standing in a slouched position. Add a reminder to your daily tasks to check in and assess whether or not you are using optimal physiology.

4. MEANING

Once something occurs in our daily life, our minds decide to give it meaning. The meaning we give it depends upon our personal life experiences, the current situation, as well as the identity traits we were born with. We discussed this concept several times throughout the book, as it is a recurring theme influencing how we think and react. Many times, the meaning we give something goes unchallenged. We accept it as a truth because this is easier for us to understand and live with. We have the power to choose what things mean to us. Through the use of words and the restructuring of our beliefs, we can redesign these meanings to help us. This is a very challenging exercise, as we will need to call out our unconscious mind and find a meaning that is better than the one we have unconsciously chosen. If the meaning we choose to use is not more powerful than the original, it will not work. The meaning we select must be more potent; it must be more advantageous for us to believe.

Sometimes things happen in life that are unfair, and in these times, it becomes extremely hard to find the meaning and to turn the situation around. For example, such things as bankruptcy, illness, death of a close friend or family member, natural disasters, or witnessing injustice can be infuriating and even debilitating. In these tough times, we can sometimes find renewed meaning in serving others, or finding ways to help the people who are affected. Recognizing that this does in fact happen to others and that you are not alone can be very therapeutic:

5. SHIFTING YOUR PERSPECTIVE

In this mind shift technique, you will see the situation through someone else's eyes. Your perspective changes when you imagine you are someone else. We have all heard the expression, "put yourself in my shoes." Well, this tool is the epitome of that. Think about what this personality would say, feel, know about, or how they would respond to your situation. You have the ability to hallucinate a bit here and try to imagine what the following personalities would say to you or how they would approach your problem. This takes a bit of work to really put yourself in character but with some practice this is an extremely powerful tool:

- God
- A wise man
- A warrior
- A magician
- A comedian
- A lover
- A child
- Someone you idolize/respect
- Your higher self
- Use your imagination; it works with anyone!

6. WORSE CASE ANALYSIS

Have you ever had a sleepless night? A night where your mind was steeped in dread and worry? Have you ever found yourself tossing and turning and walking around your home in the middle of the night thinking about problems that are stressing you out? These problems most likely relate to your interpersonal life, relationship problems, job issues, financial difficulties, and many other things you could easily worry about and stress over that keep you up all night. I'm sure

THE B.E.T.A. CYCLE

you have had a night or two of the dreaded emotion called worry. Everyone does at one time in their life. The problem is that worry and stress can eventually negatively affect you physically, emotionally and even spiritually. Stress and worry are commonplace in our society.

> *According to the American Institute of Stress, approximately "33 percent of people report feeling extreme stress. Over 77 percent of people experience stress that affects their physical health. 73 percent of people have stress that impacts their mental health." When it comes to the workplace, "80 percent of people feel stress from their jobs."*

Health professionals report that if you worry for long periods of time, it can have deleterious effects on your physical health as well. Feeling worried is a common emotion, but it is absolutely useless when it comes to helping you reach your peak potential.

With so many people feeling stress and worry, why then do experts say that 85 percent of the things we worry about actually never happen? Let's do the math! Let's say that you worry every day for seven days straight. You worry all day about something different each day. At the end of the week, you had seven solid days of worry. If 85 percent of the things you worry about "never happen" that would calculate out to 5.95 days (round it to 6 days) of things you worried about that NEVER HAPPENED! In this experiment, you really only had to choose to worry about one thing in that week. The other six days you could have been totally worry free. What if you turned those days into months, months into year, years into decades ... how much of your life did you waste dwelling on worries that never came to fruition?

You could save yourself a lot of worry if you did not worry about it.

What does this experiment mean to you? According to the math, you probably worry about 90 percent more than you should. What you worry about is 90 percent erroneous and will not happen whether you worry about it or not. You could save yourself a lot of worry if you did not worry about it.

Human beings have the unique ability to manufacture worry and stress just by making things up in our heads. Think about all those sleepless nights. By knowing 85 percent of the things you worry about never happen, you could take your sleepless nights from 100 percent of the time to 15 percent in one fell swoop. This would supply you six out of seven days of good, solid sleep, leaving you one day to worry and stay up all night. The rest of the week you can be sipping pina coladas on the beach, happy as can be (if that's your thing).

Since we have that under control, let's talk about how we can mitigate and even eliminate the stress and worry from your life.

A few years ago, I was visiting the local coffee shop where I would share pleasantries and events of the day with the barista. One day, I was particularly stressed and worried about a work situation and mentioned to her how worried I was about it. She gleefully responded, as she always does, and said,

"Oh, I was always told that 'worry' is something you <u>can't</u> do

THE B.E.T.A. CYCLE

anything about but a 'concern' is something you <u>can</u> take action on." She then asked, "Well, which one is it? Worry or concern?"

This was the best advice I had received in a long time, when I felt worried and stressed about an issue that was bothering me.

By taking the advice from the sage behind the coffee bar, the question is, "how do we put this into play?" Well, first we have to find out where worry come from? Worry is manufactured based on your *belief*, but concern is based on *evidence*. If you have a concern, you have evidence to explore in order to find solutions to the problem. With evidence, we can make decisions.

However, even if we do have concerns, we do feel uneasy about it, right? So, how do you put yourself in the state of mind that can assuage the feelings of worry, stress, and concern?

The way you do that is you ask yourself four important questions:

1. *What is the worst-case scenario?*
2. *Can I live with this worst-case scenario and can I live with the consequence?*
3. *Can I do anything about it now?*
4. *Can I do anything about it later? If so, when?*

Many times, when you ask yourself the first question, "What is the worst-case scenario?" you find that it is not nearly as bad as you thought previously. This makes you feel better instantly and gives you more hope and possibility.

If the worst-case scenario is a bad one, then you have to take the position and see if you can accept and live with the consequence. This might be difficult, but it gets you out of your head and has you think about options and other decisions you could make to solve the problem.

The next action step is to ask yourself, "Can you actually do anything about it now?" If the answer is yes, then you can begin taking steps to solve the issue. If the answer is "no" then you do not need to think about it until you need to. This is where you are able to manage your worry and concerns and focus on what you need to when you need to.

Disciplining yourself to ask these four questions when you are hit with stress, worry, and concern will help you become more efficient in solving problems, living a happier more fulfilling life, and being more effective.

> ## Expert Tip!
>
> ## Discovering the Root Cause of a Problem
>
> The first step in solving any issue is to clearly identify the problem. It should be noted that your perceived problem may be, in fact, a symptom of the actual problem and not the real issue you are wrestling with. For example, if you notice that you are starting to hate the company you have been with for the last six years, this may be a symptom but not the core issue.
>
> When you ask yourself, "What is it about the company that I hate?," you start to realize that you don't hate the company, but you really hate the fact that you were passed up for two big promotions in the past two years! Upon further questions you ask, "Why does getting passed up for two promotions bother me?" You further acknowledge that your efforts have gone unrecognized and it was really the lack of recognition and appreciation. Had your boss simply acknowledged your accomplishments and sacrifices for the company, you would be much happier. In order to discover the core issue, you can apply the same 7-Layer Exercise used in the "why" section of this book to uncover the underlying issue.

DISCOVER YOUR B.E.T.A.

In the Discovery phase, you will take an inventory of the inner workings of your mental state, the B.E.T.A Cycle (Beliefs, Emotions, Thoughts, Actions). Each quadrant of the B.E.T.A. Cycle will take you through an easy to follow, guided process to help you demystify what the heck is going on in your head. These exercises are designed to help you assess and become aware of your mindset in each of the four areas.

There are five action steps to complete in each quadrant in this exercise. The five steps are described below:

Step 1: Identify The Problem Or Issue

Write down the problem or issue that you had or are currently experiencing.

Current Problem Example: I want to run the Boston Marathon, but I am scared.

Step 2: Record Your B.E.T.A.

In the inner part of the circle, you will write in each quadrant your current Beliefs, Emotions, Thoughts, and Actions as it relates to the problem or issue.

THE B.E.T.A. CYCLE

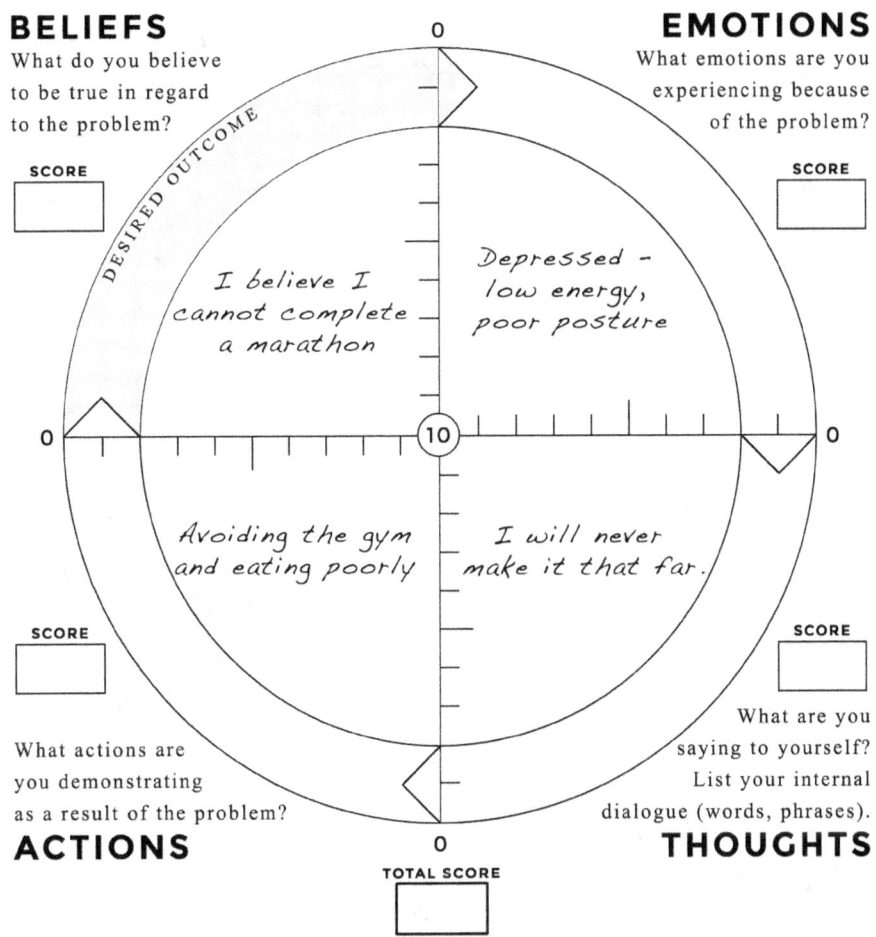

Step 3: Record Desired Outcome

In step two, in the outer circle of each quadrant, you will write your desired outcome. Your desired outcome could be the opposite of what you recorded in the inner quadrant. For example, If you stated you were "angry" in quadrant two (Emotions), you might record "happy" in the outer part of the circle. Alternatively, if you are aware of your desired outcome, write that in the outer circle.

THE MINDCOACH SYSTEM

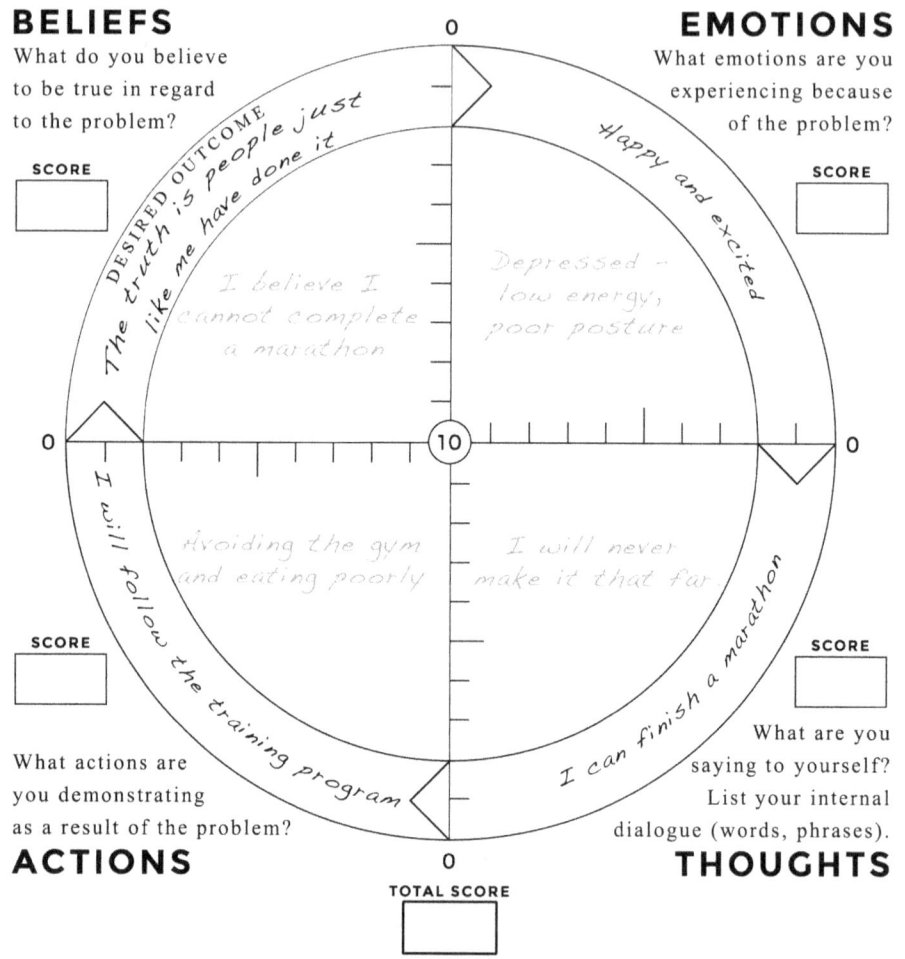

Step 4: Rate Your B.E.T.A.

In step three, you will score each of the four quadrants based on how intense you may be experiencing the Belief, Emotion, Thought, or Action. Place a mark at one of the measuring lines along the side of each quadrant. The more intense of an experience it is, the closer your mark will be to the center of the circle, which starts at 10. This is also indicative of a

THE B.E.T.A. CYCLE

closed mindset. If the Belief, Emotion, Thought, or Action is less intense, then you would mark closer to the outside of the circle, which is a 0. The outside of the circle represents an expanded mindset, which indicates fewer mental barriers, increased creativity, less stress, more confidence, and the ability to achieve your peak potential.

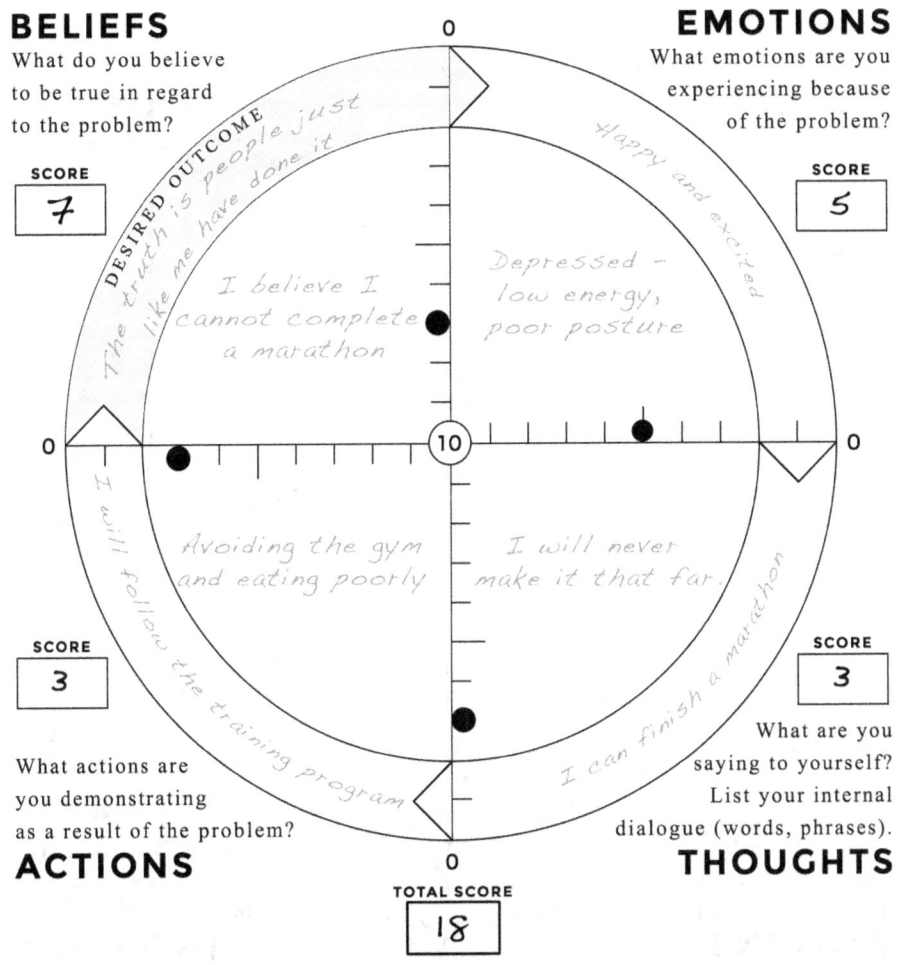

THE MINDCOACH SYSTEM

Step 5: Create Your B.E.T.A. Cycle

In step four, you will connect the dots to define your current B.E.T.A. This will give you a visual representation of your current mindset. The closer to the center of the circle you are, the more closed off your mindset is at the moment. The closer you are to the periphery of the circle, the more expansive your mindset is.

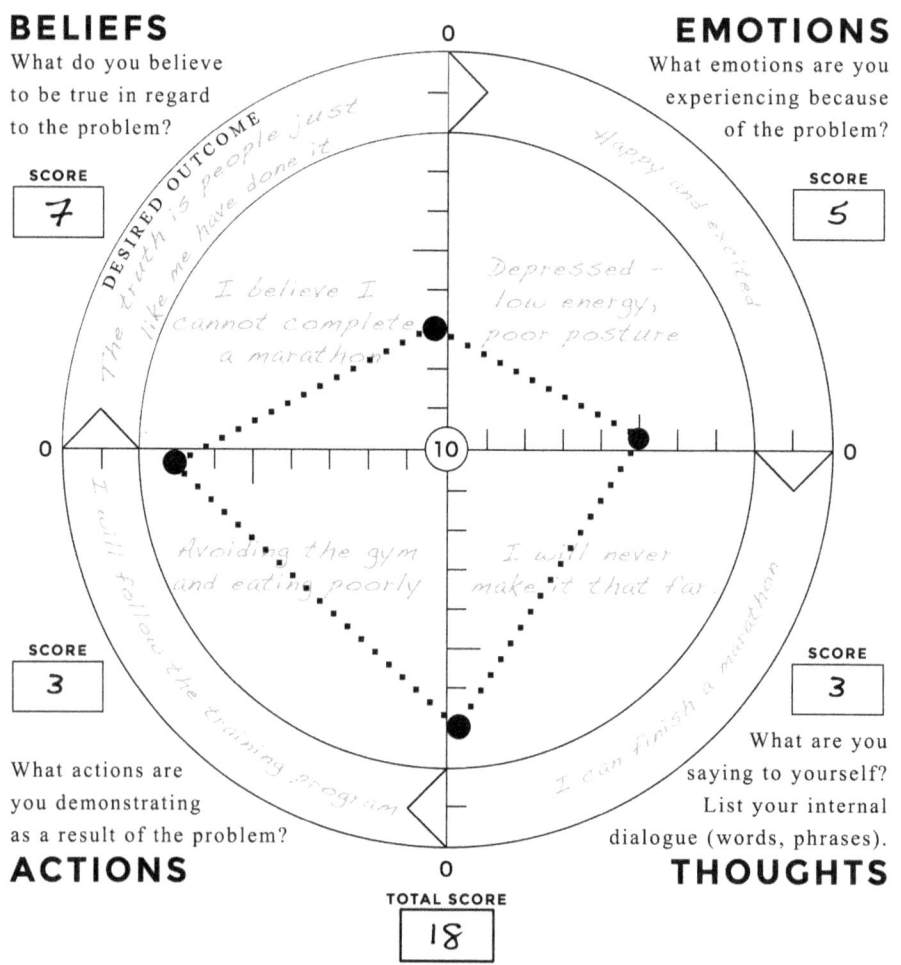

B.E.T.A. RECONSTRUCTION

In the Reconstruction phase, you will now renovate your B.E.T.A. Cycle to produce different results to reach your ultimate outcome. The way you will do this is you will reverse the cycle switching from B.E.T.A to A.T.E.B. (Actions, Thoughts, Emotions, and Beliefs). So, now as you go through the process for a second time, you will start with your actions first and then change your thoughts, which will change your emotions, and last, you will produce an alternate belief that serves your needs and goals. By switching the order of thinking, we now begin with the easiest thing to change, actions, and end with the hardest thing to change, your beliefs.

Each quadrant of the B.E.T.A. Cycle is paired with an accompanying exercise to complete. These exercises are designed to help you transform your mindset in each of the four areas. By going through this process, you will produce an unstoppable mindset and will overcome any limiting beliefs that are stopping you from reaching your peak potential.

In this part of the exercise, you will first list the "core problem" from phase 1. Next, systematically, you will proceed through the exercises outlined for each section of the B.E.T.A. Cycle starting with Actions.

ACTIONS

Changing your external actions ultimately influences and changes your internal physiology and mindset. Scientists have shown that by taking these actions a myriad of biological processes are impacted such as blood flow, blood pressure, heart rate breathing patterns, muscle tension or relaxation, and many more. As a result, this provides the resources to think more clearly and be more creative when processing your thoughts. In this section of the exercise, you will list the actions you can take and do to make these physiological processes work for you.

The first and simplest change we can make to our mindset is through altering our physiology and mindful visualization. Below is a list of activities and actions that psychologists and social science researchers have successfully used to transform a negative mindset to a positive one. The following list of actions will start the B.E.T.A. reconstruction process. Select the ones that you will commit to doing to start your transformation:

Check the actions below that you will do:

❏ Deep diaphragmatic breathing	❏ Tighten and relax muscles	❏ Stand or sit up straight
❏ Meditate	❏ Exercise	❏ Smile
❏ Create artwork	❏ Take a walk	❏ Volunteer your time to a worthy cause
❏ Write in your journal	❏ Go for a run	
❏ Do a visualization exercise	❏ Get outside into nature	❏ Spend time with friends
❏ Pray	❏ Dance	❏ Genuinely forgive someone
❏ Write down things you are grateful for	❏ Sing	❏ Have a healthy amount of sex
❏ Read an inspiring book	❏ Play an instrument	❏ Travel
	❏ Listen to music	Help someone that needs it
❏ Attend a cultural activity	❏ Eat something	
	❏ Drink water	❏ Make a phone call
❏ Set attainable goals Buy someone a gift	❏ Take a shower	❏ Compliment someone
	❏ Cook something	
	❏ Do some gardening	

Similarly, the use of visualization has also been shown to improve mood, enhance physical performance and trick the mind into seeing and feeling a result before it has actually been realized. The more clarity you are able to display during this process, the better results you will see from it. Below is another exercise we use during the BETA reconstruction phase to coax the mind into the place we desire it to go:

Visualization and Mental Rehearsal Exercise

1) Establish a highly specific goal or activity you want to achieve.
2) Imagine your future as you have already achieved it
3) Create a mental "picture."
4) Imagine it as a "movie scene" in as much detail as possible.
5) Employ all five senses in your visualization.
    i) Who are you with?
    ii) Which emotions are you feeling right now?
    iii) What are you wearing?
    iv) Is there a smell in the air?
    v) What do you hear?
6) What is your environment?
7) Sit up straight and see and feel it as the star of your action film.
8) Practice at night or in the morning (just before/after sleep).
9) Challenge and disregard any doubts if they come to you.

THOUGHTS

Changing your thoughts directly influences your emotions, both positive and negative. In the reconstruction phase, you will be altering your thoughts, internal dialogue, and mantras by establishing a statement in place of the negative one you wrote in the B.E.T.A. diagram.

Exercise:
How can you look at your current issue/situation in a more advantageous, supportive, and empowering way?

Thought	Reframe
Example: **I WILL NEVER MAKE IT THAT FAR.**	Example: **EVEN IF I DON'T FINISH, I WILL BE IN BETTER SHAPE AND HEALTHIER FOR MY FAMILY.**

EMOTIONS

The more you can separate yourself from your emotional self, the easier it will be to not judge yourself on your emotions. In other words, you are not your emotions. Your emotions are the product of your other parts of your B.E.T.A. Recognizing and knowing how you want to feel, you will be able to assess and make a conscious effort through using the tool of emotional distancing to reach the emotional state of mind you desire.

Example:

COACH: **[JOHN]** felt **[DEPRESSED]** because of **[HE FELT HE DOES NOT HAVE THE ABILITY TO RUN A MARATHON].** The emotion **[JOHN]** felt is completely normal, millions of people have felt this way before.
YOU: Because **I DON'T WANT TO DIE WITHOUT REGRETS.**
COACH: What if you were free from this emotion? How would you feel?
YOU: I now feel **MORE CONFIDENT IN MYSELF AND OPTIMISTIC ABOUT FINISHING RACE.**
COACH: What advice would your 100-year-old self give you?
YOU: My old wise self would say: **YOU CAN DO ANYTHING YOU PUT YOUR MIND TO.**
* Fill in the statement below from the conversation you had with your coach. Enter the statement below into the Emotion quadrant:
I now feel **MORE CONFIDENT THAT I CAN COMPLETE A MARATHON.**
Because **I NOW KNOW THAT I CAN DO ANYTHING I PUT MY MIND TO.**

**IMPORTANT NOTE: If you are NOT feeling better after completing this exercise, then return to the previous step and reframe your thoughts in a more advantageous and positive way. Then come back to this step once you have reconstructed your thoughts.

BELIEFS

Your beliefs are the lenses through which you see your world. In the reconstruction phase, you will challenge your belief and be able to change it so that your belief serves, not limits you. By doing this, you have more flexibility in your thinking and will be able to break through the limiting beliefs you may have that are holding you back.

> **Example:**
>
> - What would be the OPPOSITE of what you believe right now? **ENCOURAGED AND CONFIDENT**
> - Is it *REALLY* true? What hard evidence or undeniable truth do you have to support that belief? Answer: **THE TRUTH IS I CAN DO ANYTHING THAT I PUT MY MIND TO AND COMPLETE THE MARATHON.**
> - Ask yourself, "What am I afraid of that is stopping me from taking action?"
>   Answer: **I AM AFRAID TO FAIL AND FEAR THAT I WILL NOT FINISH THE RACE AND BE EMBARRASSED AND DISAPPOINTED IN MYSELF.**
> - What is an alternative belief that could also be true that you could use to replace your old belief? Answer: **PREPARING THE BEST I CAN AND GIVING EVERYTHING I HAVE WILL MAKE ME A BETTER PERSON EVEN IF I DON'T FINISH THE RACE.**
>
> **REPLACING YOUR BELIEF**
>
> The truth is:
>
> **BY SETTING THE GOAL OF RUNNING IN A MARATHON PROVIDES ME THE OPPORTUNITY TO EXPERIENCE THE EVENT AND GROW AS A PERSON EVEN IF I FINISH OR NOT.**

Reconstruct Your B.E.T.A. Cycle

As you work through the reconstruction phase, you will systematically remove the barriers that exist in your B.E.T.A.

Cycle. Within each quadrant of the diagram, you will allocate a score to your reconstructed mindset. There are 10 hash marks within each quadrant. The center of the circle indicates a score of 10. This is the most intense and restricting score. You would score yourself higher if the reconstructed solution was either ineffective or worsened your mindset in that quadrant. A lower score indicates an expanded mindset. The larger the circumference of the circle, the more progress is indicated and the closer you are to your desired state of mind. You will be able to see your progress by the differences between phase 1 and phase 2. The larger the difference, the more effective were the changes you made to your B.E.T.A. and the more expansive your mind will become as a result. The goal is to remove all restrictions with the intention of lowering your overall score to zero.

THE B.E.T.A. CYCLE

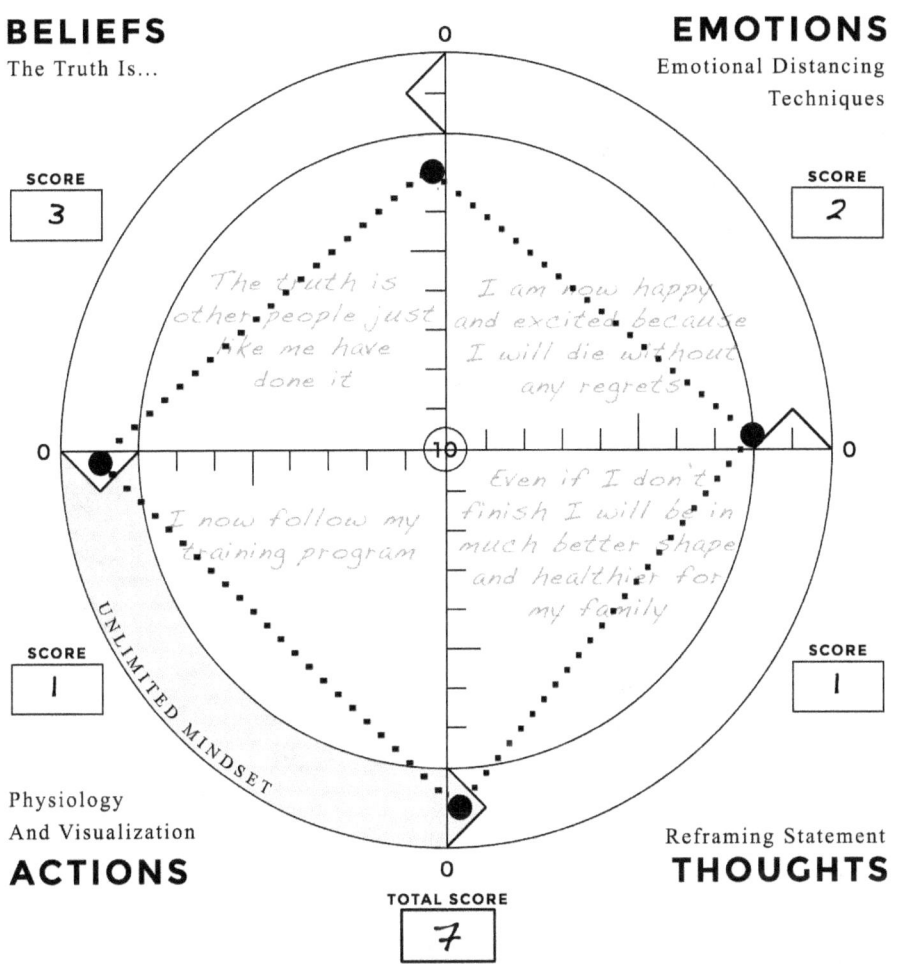

PEAK POTENTIAL

Celebrate Your Achievement And Repeat!

PEAK POTENTIAL

"Let the world know why you're here, and do it with passion."

- Wayne Dyer,
Internationally Renowned Author and Speaker in the Fields of Self-Development and Spiritual Growth

Okay, so you've done it! You are amazing! So now what?! Through your hard work, focus, and dedication, you have achieved your dream(s). This is a critical time for careful reflection, as well as celebration. Plus, it's now time to update your pyramid. Go through the 7 steps again and create an even higher peak potential for yourself. Each time you reach your peak, it naturally expands you to an even greater level of potential. In rare instances, your peak potential does have the ability to go down. This may be a health problem, or loss of certain abilities, or other external forces beyond your control. However, no matter where you are right now, aiming for the top of what you can accomplish is always a worthy endeavor. Take this time to examine what you need to stop doing, find hidden opportunities for improvement, and identify the winning patterns that got you there.

So, what does it feel like when everything is working in life and you feel great about it? Well, that is when you are in a "peak state." Some psychologists call it having a "flow" experience. Athletes say it is being in the "zone." This, however, comes with many years of working and training at their craft. They find themselves in this state of mind due to tens of thousands of hours of hard work, determination, and commitment. So, what really is this peak performance experience? It is where they are maximizing their potential and bringing the full moment into focus. It is when they are tapping into their maximum potential and are fully present in the moment. These experiences can be fleeting but they do not have to be. You don't need to work for twenty years and put in ten thousand hours of practice. By implementing the techniques and skills taught in this program, you will find your potential through being aware, assessing your thoughts and behaviors, and implementing the tools so you can take control and live the life you want.

By understanding each level of the pyramid and completing the accompanying exercises, you will have the road map to get there. As we said above, the greatest obstacle that stops us from reaching our goals and living our purpose is our mind. You now have the tools to fight back, remove the barriers that have been stopping you, and raise your peak potential even higher.

There are three things you must do after you reach the apex.

Analyze The Data

Imagine watching a baseball game, but now take away the rules of the game, the score board, the umpires, and any indicators of knowing who is winning. Not only would this game totally suck to watch, you would also never know who won. Winning at life is just like winning in any sport. First you have to understand the rules to the game you are playing as well as the underlying goals of the game. So how do you know if you are winning or have already won? Answer, you can look at the Key Performance Indicators (KPIs) that are associated with your goals. As you consistently track your progress, these indicators will tell you when you have fallen short, achieved, or surpassed your peak potential. KPIs are often used in business to track the effectiveness of a project or campaign, but they are just as effective when applied to our life goals. We pay attention to what we track. The chart below is a simple chart you can use to track your progress.

Example:

	Key Performance Indicator (KPI)	Current KPI	Target KPI
1	Number of miles I can run	3 miles	26 miles
2	Target weight for running	190 lbs	175 lbs
3			

Part of analyzing the data is also exploring what went right and what went wrong. The following are a series of powerful questions that you can ask yourself to really dig into the reasons for your success:

- What did I do well?
- What areas could I improve upon?
- What did I not do that I should have done?
- What roadblocks got in my way?
- What or who could have sped up the process?
- What did I need to stop doing?
- *Where or what do I need to focus on now to increase my peak potential?

Celebrate Your Win

First, celebrate! When you experience time at the top or achieve your goals, go ahead and treat yourself! You are doing it! It took a considerable amount of time, effort, dedication, and focus to get there, so go reap the rewards. Any great coach will reward their players or team after a stellar performance. Here, we want you to do the same. This will create a lasting feeling of fulfillment that will create even more desire for you to achieve this same result in the future. It will engrain deep in you a sense of confidence, a new identity of who you are, and a feeling of "I can do this again." So, celebrate, reward yourself, and keep working to reach your peak performance!

Below you will find a list of ways to celebrate to create powerful emotional experiences to reinforce your actions. By doing so, you will more likely aim to achieve this result again in the future.

The list below is a short compilation of ways to celebrate your achievement. Having a positive experience to look forward to helps to create additional motivation. Use your imagination to create positive emotional experiences to connect your achievement to happiness. Identify one or more celebration techniques you plan to use when you reach your peak potential:

- ❏ Write down your achievement.
- ❏ Share with others.
- ❏ Give yourself a gift.
- ❏ Treat yourself to food, snack, or a drink.
- ❏ Invite others to participate.
- ❏ Schedule a fun event.
- ❏ Write a note to someone who helped.
- ❏ Create your own power move.
- ❏ Do something you love.
- ❏ Take time off.
- ❏ Give yourself an award.
- ❏ Attend a class.
- ❏ Create a video or memoir.
- ❏ Plan a special evening.
- ❏ Reflect on your accomplishment.

Recreate The Feeling

Next, you MUST take a long, hard look at how this made you feel. Similar to muscle memory, you can coach your mind to enjoy the results that reaching your dreams provides. Try to recreate this feeling of success in your body. Your goal is to recreate the beliefs, emotions, thoughts, and actions you experienced in order to ingrain this in your subconscious. To accomplish this, you will use a powerful visualization exercise:

1. Establish a highly specific goal or activity you want to achieve.
2. Imagine the moment you experienced OR imagine a future moment to want to experience.
3. Create a mental "picture."
4. Imagine it as a "movie scene" in as much detail as possible.
5. Employ all five senses in your visualization.
   a. Who are you with?
   b. Which emotions are you feeling right now?
   c. What are you wearing?
   d. Is there a smell in the air?
   e. What do you hear?
6. What is your environment?
7. Sit up straight, add the appropriate emotion to your facial expression and see and feel it as the star of your action film.
8. Practice at night or in the morning (just before/after sleep).
9. Get rid of any doubts if they come to you.
10. Express the actual sounds, movements, and emotions out loud until you feel the result. Repeat these steps as needed to celebrate your win.

CONCLUSION

> *"The graveyard is the richest place on earth, because it is here that you will find all the hopes and dreams that were never fulfilled, the books that were never written, the songs that were never sung, the inventions that were never shared, the cures that were never discovered, all because someone was too afraid to take that first step, keep with the problem, or determined to carry out their dream."*
>
> – Les Brown, American Motivational Speaker, Author

Reaching your peak potential is an ongoing process. Striving to reach your potential takes hard work and determination, along with a strategy, planning, and a proven system. The MindCoach System offers these strategies, a plan, and a system to help you continually and consistently reach your full potential and perform at your peak. However, to do this it takes the constant focus and practice to train your mind, emotions, and body to make your dreams a reality. By following the seven-step process, you will produce greater control over your life, be more at peace and have way more fun than you ever imagined. So, when you start dreaming, don't stop. Keep dreaming and then ask why you REALLY want that in your life. After you find your reasons, set specific goals. Next, identify all the ways you can get there, and build a strategy surrounding your goals. Finally, execute on your goals and strategy with great alacrity and passion. As you follow your path to reaching your peak potential, you will constantly need to be aware of your B.E.T.A. Cycle, access it, and take immediate corrective action to coach your mind into a better place.

Similar to learning a new sport or anything new, you don't just pick it up right away. It takes practice. To apply this program, we highly recommend that you try out some of the techniques on a smaller scale. For example, you can use some of the tools outlined in this book on simple day-to-day events. For example, you wake up in the morning and check your email only to find that you have been called back into work and you were looking forward to taking the day off. This is not exactly a life-changing event, but it nonetheless has an effect on your mindset. By applying the tools from this book to an event like this, you will get better and better at turning common situations around. In this example, by going back into work you may have a chance to speak with your boss about the new raise you were trying to get. You might be able to phrase this opportunity as a way to earn more money for an upcoming trip. You can give yourself a pat on the back for being a hard worker, disciplined, and loyal to your company. There are many ways to shift your mindset so that you show up in the best form possible and remain in control of your life. On the flipside, if you do nothing about it and are angry that you need to go into work, you might take it out on the clients you are serving. You might end up getting a poor review. Your boss may see you as being resentful and unwilling to do what it takes for the company.

I encourage you to keep the MindCoach Pyramid nearby as a reminder of your commitment to reaching your potential, as well as a reminder of the fact that you have control over your mindset. Remember the best coaches are able to see things you cannot. Check in on yourself to make sure you're on track for hitting your goals. Double check yourself that you are going after the proper strategy. Hold onto the self-discipline and focus it takes to execute on the task necessary to reach your goals. And most importantly, question

CONCLUSION

your mindset often. All too often, we find ourselves in a funk, but we might go hours, days, weeks, even months not realizing that we are just running on fumes. Forcing ourselves to complete the day just so that we can do it all over again. You must have a constant reminder on you, with you, to stay on point. Look, I get it - you're probably saying to yourself right now, "I have things going on in my life that you don't understand. I like feeling crappy, just let me have my moment." Trust me, I get it more than you know and was there for a very long time. When I came to realize that although I was in my own self mourning bubble my energy and actions were inadvertently rubbing off on everyone I touched around me. Without saying anything they knew something wasn't right and ultimately what happened is they just began to feel sorry for me, pity me, and avoid interacting with me. Pretty soon I completely infected everything around me and the only thing that picked up my spirits was being around someone or something that provided a stronger emotion. When you find yourself in this place, start small. Use these tools to make a difference in other people's lives first, and what you will find is that you will begin feeling better. Revisit these tools and systems as often as necessary because you only get one chance at this amazing experience we call life.

THE MINDCOACH SYSTEM WORKBOOK

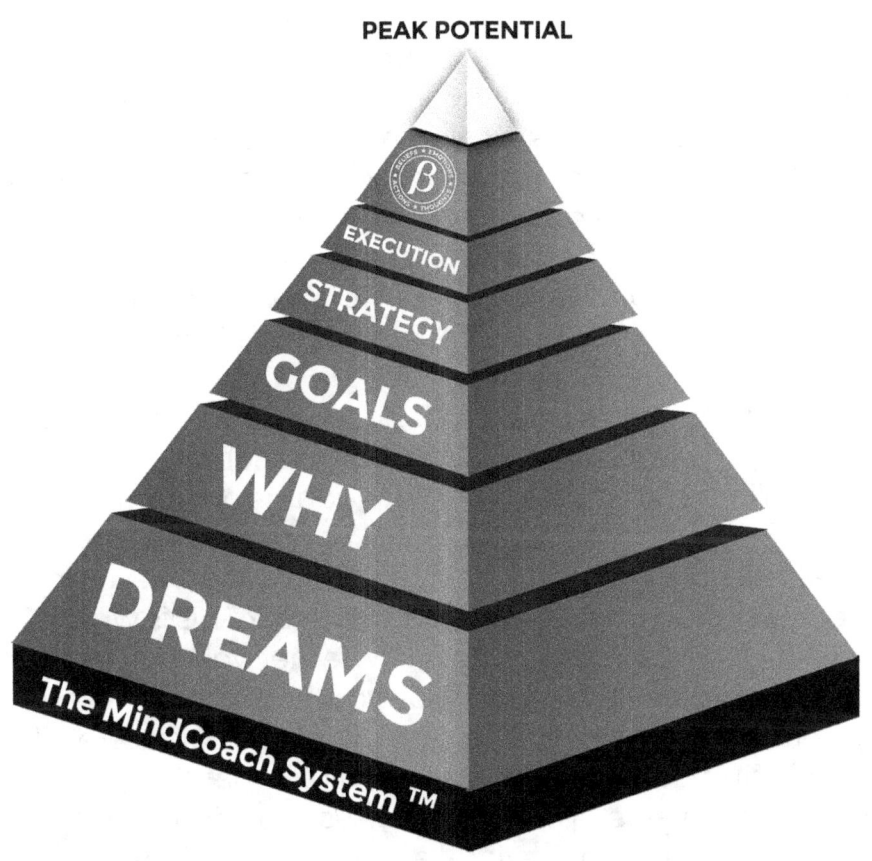

7 STEPS TO TURN DREAMS INTO REALITY

THE CHEAT SHEET FOR LIFE

Dear Friend,

I want to congratulate you and welcome you to The MindCoach Workbook. The following exercises will begin your journey toward creating a life that overflows with happiness, fulfillment, and a level of clarity few will ever experience. The fact that you made a conscious decision to participate in this program says volumes about your dedication to building a brighter future for yourself and others. I have a deep respect for you because you are clearly demonstrating a desire for inner mastery and growth. I believe wholeheartedly that following this framework will lead to a deep understanding of not only yourself but of life itself.

For several decades I have passionately sought out books, mentors, and answers to life questions that plague all of us, only to find it created even more confusion. I wondered if there was a common thread to all of this information? Was there a simple path that one can follow to achieve greater levels of success in both life and business? This is where **The MindCoach System** was born! Whether you use the exercises outlined in this system or you have similar exercises you practice to achieve the same result is completely fine. You will find that these practices will ultimately land within one of the seven steps. The exercises provided here are derived from current behavioral and sociological research and intended to accelerate your path to achieving your peak potential.

We do not know when it will be our time to part ways from this amazing world. I believe in the philosophy that we should enjoy the short amount of time that we have been blessed to spend here. It's too easy to get lost in the confusion and drift away from the essence of life itself. Use this pyramid as a way to ground yourself and bring your focus back to things that truly matter to you.

We are truly excited and privileged to share this system, which has been shaped over the past several decades. Enjoy the process but, more importantly, use it! Life can be remarkable if we only take the time and effort to make it so. How we live our life is one of the most important decisions we must make. Let's make a commitment today to start a new, exciting journey and lift yourself to a new level of passion and success. I am on this journey with you, and I cannot wait to hear about the dreams you were able to make a reality.

We wish you a fun and prosperous journey.

Now let's get started!

To your success,

Adam Kripke & David Loshelder

STEP 1: **DREAMS**

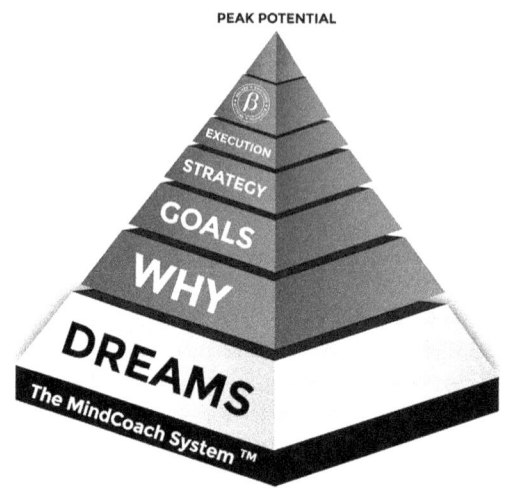

DREAM STORMING - EXERCISE 1A:

Review the categories of life listed below. Ask yourself the following questions within each category. In the next exercise, you will be writing down what comes to mind for each of the 10 categories:

10 CATEGORIES OF LIFE

Family and Home

What does your dream house look like? Where is it located?
What does your family life look like?
Recreation and fun
Where would you travel for vacation?
What activities would you do more?

Personal Growth
If you were to aim even higher, what does that dream look like for you?
What have you dreamed of learning or doing in your life?

Physical Health/Self-image
What do you want to look like?
What does a healthy lifestyle look like to you?

Spiritual
What does your spirituality look like to you?
How would you like to practice your spirituality?

Work & Career
If you could do anything and couldn't fail, what would you do?
What would you do for work?
What would you invest your time in?

Financial/Wealth
How much money would you have? What would you do with it?
Where would you invest your money?

Social Life
Who would you spend your time with?
What types of people would you love to be around?

Legacy
What does your legacy look like?

Contribution
Who or what would you support?

Use the 10 categories of life as a reference to dream storm as many things as possible that you dream about within each category. Set a timer for 30 minutes and write down your thoughts as fast as they come to you. Continue writing until the 30 minutes is up.

DREAM BOARD - EXERCISE 1B:

Again, using the 10 categories of life as well as the writing exercise above, come up with images that accurately represent your dream. You can either draw, paste, or save digital images for this exercise. Use the box below or save files to a digital device. Aim to collect 2 to 3 images for each of the 10 categories (20 to 30 images total):

DREAM BOARD - EXERCISE 1C:

Sticking these in a drawer will not get the job done. These must become a constant reminder. You may have heard the saying, "Out of sight out of mind?" Well, the only way to keep your dreams in your subconscious mind is to regularly view these images to keep your dreams in focus.

Here are a few suggestions to keep your dreams top of mind:

- **SCREENSAVER** - Next, save all your images into a folder on your computer or digital device called "Dream Board." Next, go to your screensaver setting and make these images appear as your screensaver. Voila! Now you have an ongoing reminder of where you want to go.
- **VISION BOARD** - Print off your images and paste or pin them onto a wall or cork board that is viewed regularly.
- **DREAM BOOK** - Create a small scrapbook or album that you can look at often.
- **BACKGROUND IMAGES** - Take your images and turn them into your digital background on any of your digital devices.
- **SHARE WITH FRIENDS** - Create an album online or share images with your friends on social media.
- **MAKE A VIDEO** - Convert your images into a compelling video. Add music, voice over, or other dimensions to strengthen its appeal.

STEP 2: **WHY**

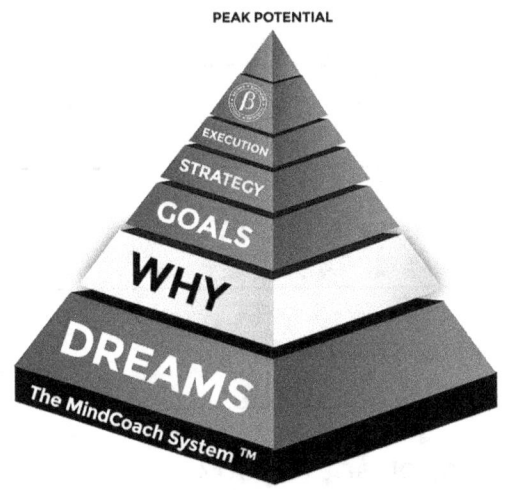

PEEL BACK THE LAYERS - EXERCISE 2:

In this exercise, you will ask yourself why you REALLY want the dreams you identified. Take a hard look at all your dreams. Select one dream you wish to come true.

Ask yourself the following questions with the intention of going deeper into your "why" as you go. The purpose here is to become more self-aware. Keep in mind that your dreams tie back to an emotion or feeling you want. So, make note of those feelings as you work through this exercise. These feelings are the forces that pull you to your peak potential as you work through the program:

Your Dream:
_____
_____
_____

1.) What is important to you about realizing this dream?
_____

2.) Why is that important to you?
_____

3.) Why is that important to you?
_____

4.) Why is that important to you?
_____

5.) Why is that important to you?
_____

6.) Why is that important to you?
_____

7.) Why is that important to you?**
_____

(Use this last "why" when writing your goals in the next step)

STEP 3: **GOALS**

D.I.B.B.S. (DREAMS - I WILL - BY - BECAUSE - STRATEGY) - EXERCISE 3:

You will now take your most important dream and create a specific goal for it. Every goal will include three main components: (1) what you want, which is the dream you wish to accomplish, (2) when you want it, and (3) why you want it. *When filling in your "because" part of your goal, use the last reason "why" you listed in the "peeling back the layers" in exercise 2.* When writing down your goals, we are only looking to clarify the desired end destination.

Goal template:

I will: *[insert your dream here]*

By: *[insert timeline here]*

Because: *[insert your reason why here].*

Goal Example:

I will Run the Boston Marathon

By March 2022

Because: I do not want to die without any regrets!

Write YOUR Goal:

I will:
_____

By:
_____

Because:
_____

**In the next step we will create a strategy to accomplish your goal.

STEP 4: **STRATEGY**

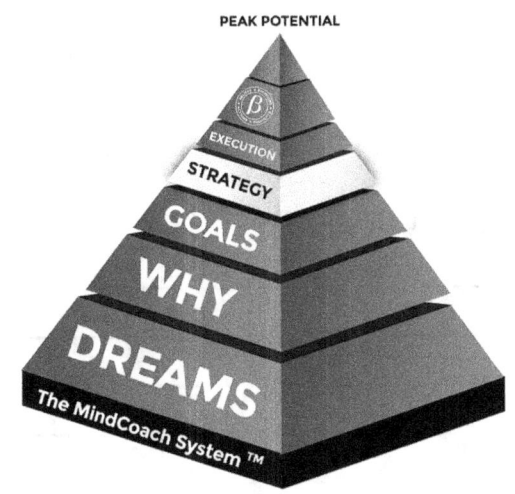

DEFINE THE PROBLEM - EXERCISE 4A:

There are four parts to building in effective strategy. Number one, you first need to define the problem you are trying to solve. The challenge to this exercise is first coming up with the right problem you are trying to solve. In this exercise you will write down your problem in multiple ways using different words and desired outcomes in order to produce new and innovative solutions.

Problem Example: *I must significantly improve my diet, overall strength, and cardiovascular stamina in order to run the Boston Marathon.*

Problem To Solve (Version 1)

_____

_____

Problem To Solve (Version 2)

_____
_____
_____
_____

Problem To Solve (Version 3)

_____
_____
_____
_____

CREATE A STRATEGY FILTER - EXERCISE 4B:

Next you will need to create a filter. By creating a filter, you can quickly identify the best options that exist to accomplish your goals. In essence you are specifying criteria that must be met in order for the strategies you identify to be considered as a solution to your problem. What MUST your solutions include? Create your list of criteria below. Before you choose strategy to implement, make sure to cross-reference it with your filter and check the boxes of the ones that match. Disregard anything that does not meet your requirements.

Problem Example: *I must significantly improve my diet, overall strength, and cardiovascular stamina in order to run the Boston Marathon.*

Strategy Filter Example:

❏ Must be a vegan diet

- ❏ The training must be easy on my knees
- ❏ Must be able to train early in the morning
- ❏ The trainer must have experience training elite runners
- ❏ The trainer must be officially certified and insured

Your Problem To Solve:

_____

_____

Your Strategy Filter:

❏ _____

❏ _____

❏ _____

❏ _____

❏ _____

❏ _____

❏ _____

❏ _____

❏ _____

❏ _____

THE MINDCOACH MATRIX - EXERCISE 4C:

In step three it's time to get resourceful. Here you will take an inventory of everything you have access to. This is a powerful creative thinking exercise and does require a considerable amount of internal and external investigation. The purpose here is to pioneer more effective ways to reach your dreams. There are no wrong answers.

How To Use The MindCoach Matrix:

Start on the left side at the top with "You." Then match the word on the left with the first word on the top, "Assets." In the intersecting cell of the chart, you will brainstorm and write down ALL the "Assets" that "You" have. Once completed move onto the second word on the top, "Products." Name all the "Products" that "You" can leverage. Continue down the chart until you complete the row. Then move onto the next row, "family." Write down everything that your family may have access to and so on. Repeat this process until the chart is filled in. You can download an editable version of the MindCoach Matrix at www.mindcoachsystem.com. Otherwise you can create a spreadsheet of your own, create a mindmap, or write down your findings:

THE MINDCOACH SYSTEM WORKBOOK

MINDCOACH MATRIX

	You	Family	Friends	People	Professionals	Companies	Educational Institutions	Government	Environmt
Assets									
Products									
Services									
Barter									
Skills									
Technology									
Relationships									
Collaborations									
Distribution									
Opportunities									
Activities									
Events									
Systems									
Acquisitions									

MEMORY HELPER

Use this sheet to help you think about who you may know. Many times, the strategy we are trying to find is less about how to do something and more about who can help:

Coworker	Principal	Church leadership	Firefighter
Boss	Teacher	Church volunteers	Scout leader
Employee partner	Coach	Churchgoers	Auctioneer
Janitor	Gym	Carpool	Photographer
Security guard	Therapist	Yoga	Guidance counselor
Delivery person	Hairdresser	Pilates	Musician
Mail person	Carpenter	PTA	Farmer
Administrative staff	Car mechanic	Hometown	Military
Customer	Salesperson	School reunion	Babysitter
Parking attendant	Gas station	Colleges	Parents
Landscaper	Police officer	Daycare Center	Neighbors
Coffee shop	Painter	Park	Best man
Manager	Roofer	Has a truck	Maid of honor
Competition	Bookstore	Plays an instrument	Bridesmaids
Repair person	Department store	Lifts weights	Groomsmen
Repair company	Grocery store	Little League	Singers
Nephew	Waiter or waitress	YMCA	Plumber
Niece	Restaurant	Apartment manager	Sports teams
Best friend	Convenient store	Chiropractor	Local celebrities
Delivery person	Chef	Professor	Local radio
Ex-company	Cashier	Preacher	From out of state
Ex-boss	Dishwasher	Nurse	From out of country
Job hunters	Hardware store	Dentist	Land
New employee	Truck driver	Doctor	Buildings
Operator	Pharmacist	Mortgage broker	Inventions
Payroll	Flower shop	Landlord	Documents
Contractor	Health spa	Nonprofits	Skills
Clients	Fast food restaurants	Associations	Podcasts
Sister-in-law Brother-in-law Father-in-law	Toy store	Social media groups	Past celebrities
	Fabric store	Influencers	Past leaders
Mother-in-law	Dry cleaner	Workshops	Events
Brother	Students	Seminars	Utility providers
Sister	Repair person	Certifications	Restaurant
Father	Theater	Software engineers	Inspector
Mother	Realtor	Website designers	Banker
Grandparents	Office supplies	App developers	Magazines
Cousin	Pizza delivery	Manufacturers	Newsletters
Aunt	Phone installer	Kids	Yellow pages
Uncle	Pest control	Pet groomers	TV shows
Past Roommate	Landscaper	Pet stores	Books
	Engineer	Veterinarians	
		Cemeteries	

CREATE A WINNING COMBINATION - EXERCISE 4D:

You've created a list of your resources and have expanded your options. It's now time to create a winning combination. You now have everything you need to build a winning strategy. All you have to do is now line them up in an order that expedites your success. For the sake of simplicity, you will design a three-step strategy using the template below:

Initial Action	Primary Action	Final Action
Identify the initial tasks you can do to start you on the path to achieving your dream. In the first column insert all the tasks or steps that you could do as the initial move.	What is your main objective? What is the primary task, action, or step you want to have happen? In the second column list all your primary actions.	What are the last steps in your winning combination? What things could be done that would solidify your path to achieve your dreams? How can you make it last longer? Enter these in the last column.

EXAMPLE:

Initial Action	Primary Action	Final Action
• Research personal trainers • Hire a nutritionist • Speak with my friend Mark who ran the Boston Marathon • Contact Samantha to be my training partner	• Complete weekly training plan • Record nutrition • Track improvements and progress in running journal • Schedule bi-weekly massage	• Run Boston Marathon • Maintain nutritional changes • Celebrate your success! • Buy Samantha a gift • Continue off-season training

YOUR WINNING COMBINATION

Initial Action	Primary Action	Final Action

STEP 5: **EXECUTION**

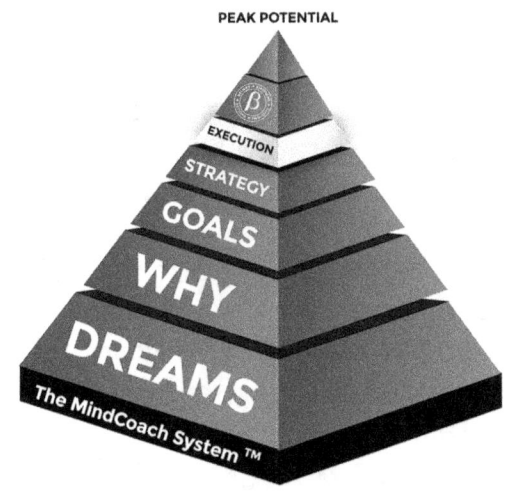

PRIORITIZE YOUR TASKS - EXERCISE 5A:

It's time to get stuff done! In the previous strategy exercise you identified steps that will get you closer to reaching your goals. It's very easy to get lost in the shuffle of everyday life and lose sight of our dreams and goals. In this simple exercise you will <u>select two tasks each day to complete</u>. How you choose to incorporate this into your day is completely up to you. If you complete these tasks, it not only moves you closer to achieving your dreams but it also gives you a satisfying sense of progress and accomplishment. Review your goal as well as the strategies you wrote down to guide you in determining what tasks to execute. In addition, you can ask yourself the following questions to further assist you to vet the tasks you place on your daily list:

1. What is the number one thing you MUST do for yourself or your business in the next twelve months to get you

much closer to your goal(s)?

2. What are the top three tasks you MUST do NOW that will move you closer to your goals?

3. What tasks would you consider to be the low-hanging fruit? Which ones are more likely to be successful, profitable, and easier to execute?

Helpful Tips: *When writing your task(s) use an action word or phrase, for example "write email," "call John," "order product," "verify product," "Thank John," etc.*

Example Daily Tasks:

1. Contact John, my personal trainer, and schedule an appointment to review my goal to run the Boston Marathon.

2. Throw away my large stash of delicious candy I hid in the kitchen cabinet above the oven. Begin cutting out sugar from my diet today.

Write down the top 2 things you must do today:
DAILY TASKS
1. _____
_____
_____
2. _____
_____
_____

DEVELOP NEW HABITS AND ROUTINES - EXERCISE 5B

Write in the habits at the top of the sheet. Place a checkmark in the box of the habits you successfully accomplished for each day of the month that day. Aim to get a minimum of three habits for each day. Keep this worksheet somewhere where you will see it each night. Update this sheet with your accomplishments for the day. Print off a new sheet for each month.

Example:

	Habit 1 Relationships	Habit 2 Health & Fitness	Habit 3 Creativity	Habit 4 Build Knowledge	Habit 5 Evolve Mindset
Month: JANUARY	Contact 5 people every day	Exercise for 20 minutes	Write in my journal	Read for 30 minutes	Meditate for 5 minutes
1	✓	✓	X	✓	X
2					

Use the following worksheet to implement new habits. Enter in a maximum of five habits you either must stop doing OR habits you must start doing to reach your dream. The best way to do this is to replace a bad habit with a good habit. By replacing unfavorable habits with favorable ones, you will focus on the habits you want to cement into your daily life. To download a copy of the Habit Forming Worksheet go to www.mindcoachsystem.com.

THE MINDCOACH SYSTEM

	Habit 1 Relationships	Habit 2 Health & Fitness	Habit 3 Creativity	Habit 4 Build Knowledge	Habit 5 Evolve Mindset
Month :					
1					
2					
3					
4					
5					
6					
7					
8					
9					
10					
11					
12					
13					
14					
15					
16					
17					
18					
19					
20					
21					
22					
23					
24					
25					
26					
27					
28					
29					
30					
31					

SCHEDULED REST AND RECOVERY - EXERCISE 5C

Scheduling time for rest and recovery will not only help you to be less stressed but will also make you more productive throughout your day. When filling out your habits, add one or more of the rest and recovery techniques below to your day. You will notice many of the techniques mention being "mindful" during the technique. This means you will aim to focus your awareness on the present moment, in a meditative like manner. The objective here is to shift our thinking into the present moment of what we are currently doing instead of focusing on the past or the future. Which of the following rest and recovery techniques will you add to your weekly schedule? Place a checkmark next to the techniques you plan to utilize. Then write in three techniques you plan to do:

Which rest and recovery technique will you implement?	
❑ Meditation ❑ Positive affirmations ❑ Guided visualization ❑ Journaling ❑ Calming arts and crafts projects ❑ Diaphragmatic breathing techniques ❑ Mindful eating	❑ Mindful movement (Yoga, Qigong, Tai Chi, Silat Tuo, etc.) ❑ Mindful exercise ❑ Mindful bodywork (massage, acupuncture, trigger point therapy, etc.) ❑ Taking a mental break ❑ Spend time outside in nature ❑ New experiences

Rest and Recovery #1:	
Rest and Recovery #2:	
Rest and Recovery #3:	

STEP 6: **B.E.T.A. CYCLE**

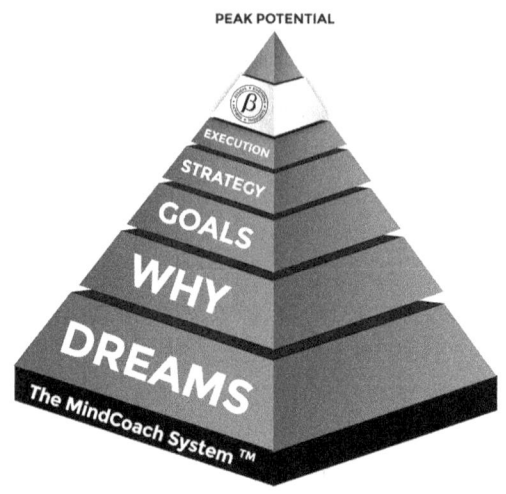

In the first phase of this exercise, we will first help you discover your hidden mindset and extract the beliefs, emotions, thoughts, and actions that are holding you back from reaching your peak potential. Next, in phase two you will reconstruct your B.E.T.A. Cycle into one that supports your dreams and expands your possibilities.

PHASE 1

B.E.T.A. CYCLE DISCOVERY

DISCOVER YOUR B.E.T.A. CYCLE - EXERCISE 6A:

In Phase 1 of the B.E.T.A. Cycle, you will perform four action steps:

1. IDENTIFY THE PROBLEM: First you write down the problem you are experiencing.

Questions To Ask Yourself:

What generated the thought, feeling or behavior?

- Environment?
- Self?
- People?

How was your thought, feeling, or behavior triggered? What was the exact trigger?

Where is this conflict coming from? Which of these is it in conflict with?

- Your core values?
- Your core beliefs?
- The identity you have of yourself?

When & where did this internal conflict originate from?

- Past history?
- Present?
- Future (i.e., fears, anxiety, excitement, etc.)?

2. ANSWER THE QUESTIONS: Answer the questions listed in each of the four quadrants relating to your beliefs, emotions, thoughts, and actions and write it in the circle. Start with your beliefs and continue in a clockwise manner, finishing with actions.

3. RATE THE INTENSITY: Mark the intensity of each B.E.T.A. on the hash marks in each quadrant. The center of the circle is a 10, most intense, and at the outer edge of the circle is an intensity score of 0.

4. TOTAL YOUR SCORE: Add up the number in each

quadrant to calculate your total score. This number is your base "Mindset Growth Score."

Example:

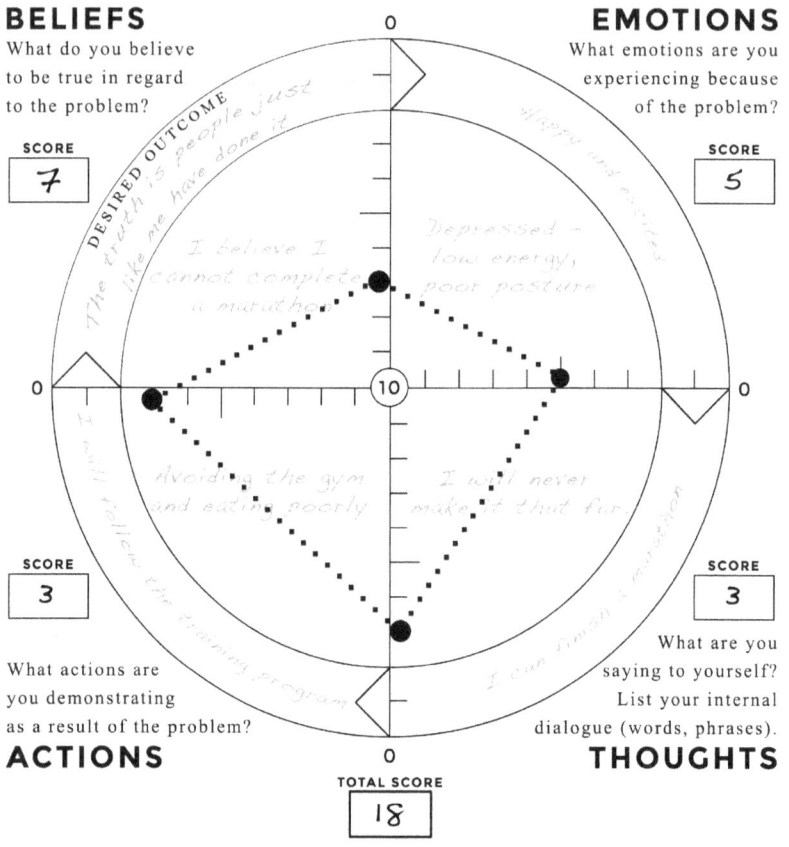

	DISCOVERY SCORE		RECONSTRUCTION SCORE		MINDSET GROWTH TOTAL
BELIEFS	7	−		=	
EMOTIONS	5	−		=	
THOUGHTS	3	−		=	
ACTION	3	−		=	
TOTAL	18	−		=	

THE MINDCOACH SYSTEM WORKBOOK

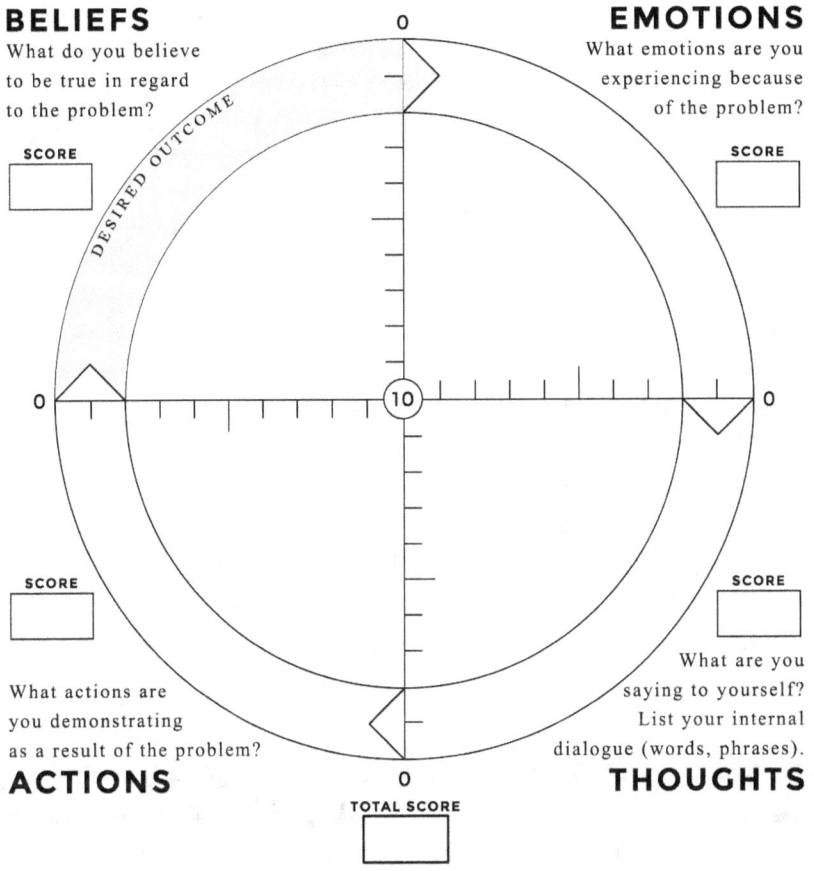

BELIEFS
What do you believe to be true in regard to the problem?

SCORE

EMOTIONS
What emotions are you experiencing because of the problem?

SCORE

SCORE

SCORE

ACTIONS
What actions are you demonstrating as a result of the problem?

What are you saying to yourself? List your internal dialogue (words, phrases).
THOUGHTS

TOTAL SCORE

	DISCOVERY SCORE		RECONSTRUCTION SCORE		MINDSET GROWTH TOTAL
BELIEFS		−		=	
EMOTIONS		−		=	
THOUGHTS		−		=	
ACTION		−		=	
TOTAL		−		=	

Reconstructing your mindset is a challenging but wildly rewarding process. It starts by completing the following exercises within each of the four quadrants for Beliefs, Emotions, Thoughts, and Actions. Similar to the previous section, you will enter the answers of the exercises into the corresponding quadrants and score your results. Read through the following exercises before completing the B.E.T.A. Reconstruction at the end of this section.

1. Actions

CHANGE YOUR PHYSIOLOGY - EXERCISE 6B:

The first and simplest change we can make to our mindset is through altering our physiology. Remember, emotions are physiological in nature so by participating in certain activities it will simultaneously impact mood. Below is a list of things that psychologists and social science researchers have found to make a shift to a long-lasting positive mindset.

Check the actions below that you will do:

- ☐ Deep diaphragmatic breathing
- ☐ Meditate
- ☐ Create artwork
- ☐ Write in your journal
- ☐ Do a visualization exercise
- ☐ Pray
- ☐ Write down things you are grateful for
- ☐ Read an inspiring book
- ☐ Attend a cultural activity
- ☐ Set attainable goals Buy someone a gift
- ☐ Tighten and relax muscles
- ☐ Exercise
- ☐ Take a walk
- ☐ Go for a run
- ☐ Get outside into nature
- ☐ Dance
- ☐ Sing
- ☐ Play an instrument
- ☐ Listen to music
- ☐ Eat something
- ☐ Drink water
- ☐ Take a shower
- ☐ Cook something
- ☐ Do some gardening
- ☐ Stand or sit up straight
- ☐ Smile
- ☐ Volunteer your time to a worthy cause
- ☐ Spend time with friends
- ☐ Genuinely forgive someone
- ☐ Have a healthy amount of sex
- ☐ Travel Help someone that needs it
- ☐ Make a phone call
- ☐ Compliment someone

VISUALIZATION - EXERCISE 6C:

Using visualization is a persuasive technique to effectuate change in your mind. There are an infinite number of ways to practice visualization. Below is a simple process to follow to start this useful practice:

Visualization and Mental Rehearsal Exercise

1. Establish a highly specific goal or activity you want to achieve.
2. Imagine your future as you have already achieved it.
3. Create a mental "picture."
4. Imagine it as a "movie scene" in as much detail as possible.
5. Employ all five senses in your visualization.
   a. Who are you with?
   b. Which emotions are you feeling right now?
   c. What are you wearing?
   d. Is there a smell in the air?
   e. What do you hear?
6. What is your environment?
7. Sit up straight and see and feel it as the star of your action film.
8. Practice at night or in the morning (just before/after sleep).
9. Challenge and disregard any doubts if they come to you.

---

2. Thoughts

To create new and empowering thoughts, we will use a mental modification process. In this exercise you will be guided through a reframing process to generate new thought patterns to achieve your desired outcome. You must reframe the negative thought to one that is advantageous for you. Find a new and empowering meaning that can equally be true to transform the negative thought into a positive one:

REFRAMING - EXERCISE 6D:

How can you look at your current issue/situation in a more advantageous, supportive, and empowering way?	
Thought	Reframe
Example: I paid more taxes this year than last year!	Example: I made more money this year than last year.

3. Emotions

EMOTIONAL DISTANCING - EXERCISE 6E:

With this technique, you will talk and see yourself in the third person. This will give you the ability to distance yourself from the emotion/feeling you are experiencing and subsequently provide you with the ability to not only change your feeling to a more advantageous one but also weaken the intensity the emotion has on your mind. Think of this as a dialogue you are having with the most knowledgeable and motivational coach in history:

THE MINDCOACH SYSTEM WORKBOOK

COACH: [your first name] felt **[emotion]** because of **[your triggering event]**. The emotion **[your first name]** felt is completely normal, millions of people have felt this way before. What is your reason for getting rid of this emotion?
YOU: Because _____
COACH: *OK, now how would you feel right now if the emotion were gone?*
YOU: I now feel _____
COACH: What advice would your 100-year-old self give you in this moment?
YOU: My old wise self would say:
_____
_____

* Fill in the statement below from the conversation you had with your coach. Enter the statement below into the Emotion quadrant:
I now feel _____
Because _____

IMPORTANT NOTE: *If you are NOT feeling better after completing this exercise, then return to the previous step and reframe your thoughts in a more advantageous and positive way. Then come back to this step once you have reconstructed your thoughts.*

4. BELIEFS

CHALLENGE YOUR BELIEF - EXERCISE 6F:

It's time to create a new belief to replace your old limiting one. The following questions will help to generate new perspectives and challenge your current beliefs. After completing the probing questions, fill in the statement that you will adopt as your new truth. Fill in the blank after "the truth is" to solidify your new belief. Enter this phrase into your B.E.T.A. Reconstruction:

- What would be the OPPOSITE of what you believe right now?
- Is it *REALLY* true? What hard evidence or undeniable truth do you have to support that belief?
  Answer:_____

- Ask yourself, "What am I afraid of that is stopping me from taking action?"
  Answer:_____

- What is an alternative belief that could also be true that you could use to replace your old belief?
  Answer:_____

REPLACING YOUR BELIEF

The truth is: _____

B.E.T.A. RECONSTRUCTION- EXERCISE 6G:

Here you will enter the answers you came up with in the previous exercises and place them into their corresponding quadrant.

1. **ANSWER THE QUESTIONS**: Answer the questions listed in each of the four quadrants relating to your beliefs, emotions, thoughts, and actions and write them in the inner circle. Start with your beliefs and continue in a clockwise manner, finishing with actions.
2. **RATE THE INTENSITY**: Mark the intensity of each B.E.T.A. on the hash marks in each quadrant. The intensity is measured as the following: (1 current mindset and 10 desired mindset).
3. **TOTAL YOUR SCORE**: Add up the number in each quadrant to calculate your total score. This number is your base "Mindset Growth Score."

**Repeat this practice each time you discover a limiting belief, emotion, thought, or action occurring. The more you practice the BETA Reconstruction, the better you will become at coaching your mind.

THE MINDCOACH SYSTEM

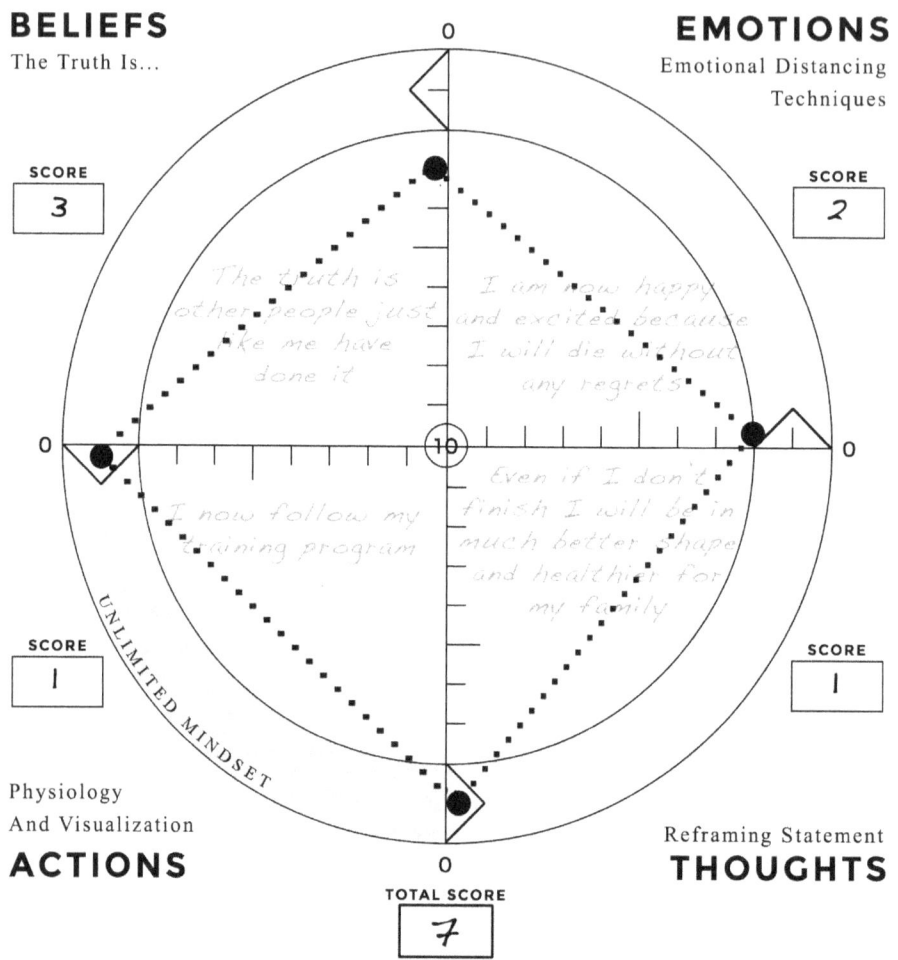

	DISCOVERY SCORE		RECONSTRUCTION SCORE		MINDSET GROWTH TOTAL
BELIEFS	7	-	3	=	4
EMOTIONS	5	-	2	=	3
THOUGHTS	3	-	1	=	2
ACTION	3	-	1	=	2
TOTAL	18	-	7	=	11

THE MINDCOACH SYSTEM WORKBOOK

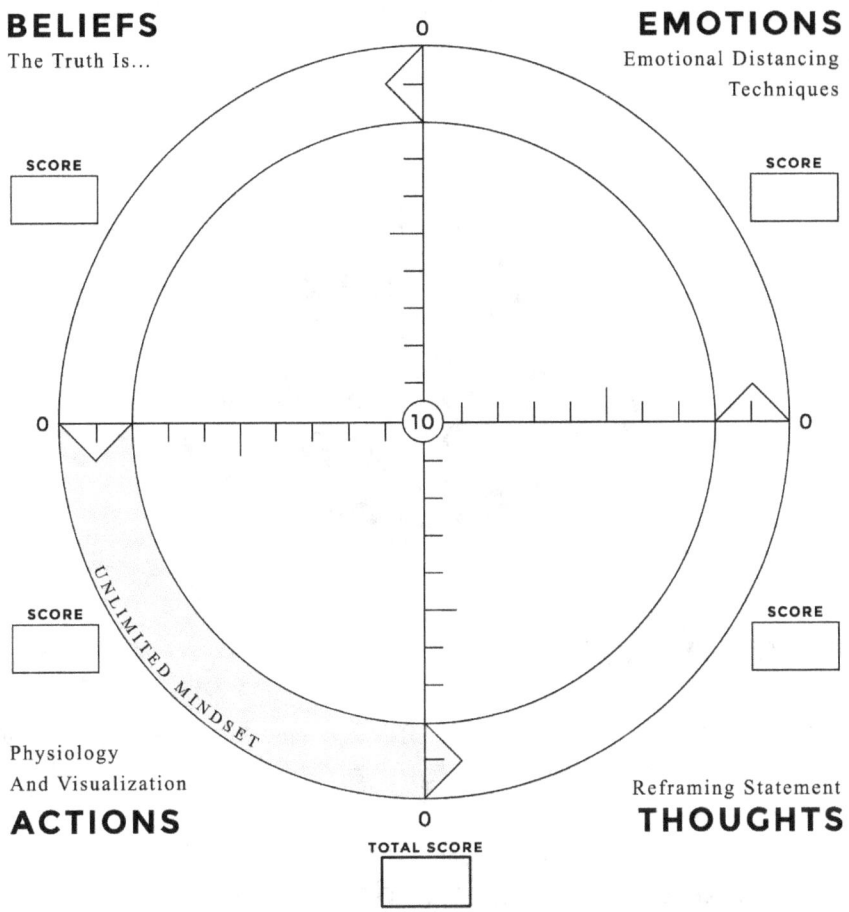

	DISCOVERY SCORE		RECONSTRUCTION SCORE		MINDSET GROWTH TOTAL
BELIEFS		−		=	
EMOTIONS		−		=	
THOUGHTS		−		=	
ACTION		−		=	
TOTAL		−		=	

STEP 7: **PEAK POTENTIAL**

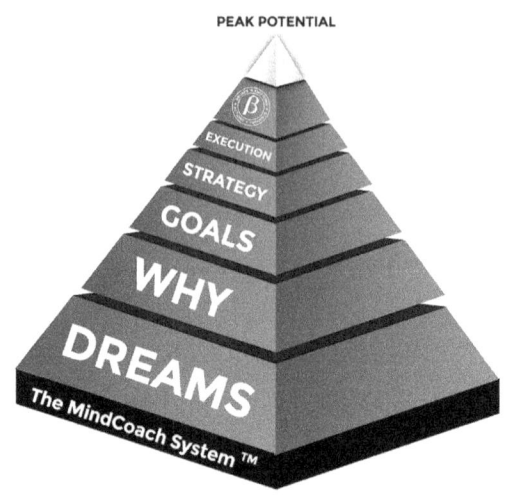

ANALYZE THE DATA - EXERCISE 7A:

In order to determine if you are winning or have won, you must know the score of the game. This is your score board. Use the chart below to identify the key performance indicators (KPIs) that directly relate to your goal. Write down your top three KPIs below. Also include where you are now in the current KPI column. Next write down your target KPI in the last column:

Key Performance Indicators (KPI)	Current KPI	Target KPI
1		
2		
3		

Q: What did I do well?
_____
_____

Q: What areas could I improve upon?
_____
_____

Q: What did I not do that I should have done?
_____
_____

Q: What roadblocks got in my way?
_____
_____

Q: What or who could have sped the process up?
_____
_____

Q: What did I need to stop doing?
_____
_____

Q: *Where or what do I need to focus on now to increase my peak potential?
_____
_____

CELEBRATE YOUR WIN - EXERCISE 7B:

Time to celebrate! Select one or more of the celebration techniques from the list below to perform with yourself and or others:

☐ Write down your achievement. ☐ Share with others. ☐ Give yourself a gift. ☐ Treat yourself to food, snack, or a drink. ☐ Invite others to participate. ☐ Schedule a fun event. ☐ Write a note to someone who helped	☐ Create your own power move. ☐ Do something you love. ☐ Take time off. ☐ Give yourself an award. ☐ Attend a class. ☐ Create a video or memoir. ☐ Plan a special evening. ☐ Reflect on your accomplishment.

Celebration #1:	
Celebration #2:	
Celebration #3:	

RECREATE THE FEELING - EXERCISE 7C:

Your goal here is to recreate the beliefs, emotions, thoughts, and actions you experienced in order to engrain this into your subconscious. By giving yourself this gift, you will program your mind to enjoy how reaching your dream made you feel. Complete the visualization process below to reward your mind:

1. Establish a highly specific goal or activity you want to achieve.
2. Imagine the moment you experienced OR imagine a future moment to want to experience.
3. Create a mental "picture."

4. Imagine it as a "movie scene" in as much detail as possible.
5. Employ all five senses in your visualization.
   a. Who are you with?
   b. Which emotions are you feeling right now?
   c. What are you wearing?
   d. Is there a smell in the air?
   e. What do you hear?
6. What is your environment?
7. Sit up straight, add the appropriate emotion to your facial expression and see and feel it as the star of your action film.
8. Practice at night or in the morning (just before/after sleep).
9. Get rid of any doubts if they come to you.
10. Express the actual sounds, movements, and emotions out loud until you feel the result. Repeat these steps as needed to celebrate your win.

THE MINDCOACH SYSTEM POSTER

The MindCoach Poster will help you to keep your plan top of mind. You can go to www.mindcoachsystem.com to print this off for yourself. Fill in the sections of the pyramid to provide yourself with a constant reminder of your progress and success.

THE MINDCOACH SYSTEM

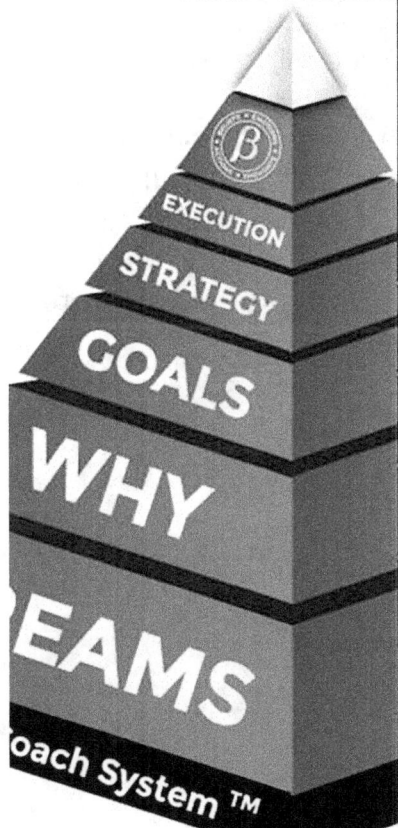

STEP 1: DREAM - What do you dream about?

STEP 2: WHY - Why is this important to you?

STEP 3: GOAL - What goals do you need to set to accomplish it?
I will: _____

By: _____
Because: _____

STEP 4: EXECUTION - Take action and create new habits.

STEP 5: STRATEGY - What options do you have? Who can help?

STEP 6: B.E.T.A. CYCLE - Reconstruct your Beliefs, Emotions, Thoughts, and Actions.

STEP 7: PEAK POTENTIAL - Measure and celebrate!

Key Performance Indicators (KPIs)	Current KPI	Target KPI
1		
2		
3		

SUMMARY

Since you have celebrated your success, now it is time to visit your Dream Board once again! Go back and choose three more dreams from your Dream Board. Start the process as you did in your first go-around. If you have other dreams you would like to add, go ahead and add them to the board. Life is cyclical, and each time you round the turn, you find yourself in a better place than you did before you started. Each time you go through The MindCoach System, you will find that your ability to do more, be more, and become more increases in capacity. Reaching your peak potential takes hard work. As you most likely noticed, if you follow the steps, work through them, stay diligent, and stay focused, you will find that the system gives you all that you need to live the life you desire and deserve. Do not give up until you are insanely proud of yourself. Stay on the road to becoming the best version of yourself, my friend. There is no better path in life worth traveling.

ABOUT THE AUTHORS

Adam Kripke

Adam has captured the respect and attention of CEOs, entrepreneurs, and marketing experts because of his unique ability to effortlessly connect invisible dots and to identify innovative yet simple solutions that most business owners never see.

Not only does he have the ability to think WAY outside the box, but he also can think way inside the box as well. This is a result of Adam's extensive cross-industry knowledge from having owned and operated, worked in, or been deeply affiliated with 100+ industries and subindustries in his lifetime. Adam has participated in 500+ individual projects totaling in excess of $5 billion dollars. In addition to graduating with a B.S. from Colorado State University, more notably Adam graduated from several alternative educational institutions including mentoring and training from four of the most prestigious thought leaders in the world.

Adam is the founder & CEO of Alpha Project, a mastermind consultancy and joint venture marketing company, and owns numerous real estate investment companies. Over the past 20 years, he built 17 diverse companies. Adam was an area developer, business consultant, and master franchise for Cold Stone Creamery. Adam and his team were awarded the *Area Developer Of The Year Award* and *Top Dollar Club Award* for being one of the top 50 highest grossing ice cream stores in the world.

Adam also co-founded the LSI Group, an international consultancy that facilitated business development, collaborations, and joint ventures between Indonesia and the United States.

Adam lives for creating breakthroughs, stimulating conversation, personal growth, and seeing the smiles of business owners after making a massive breakthrough that will transform their life and business. He is an avid skier and kiteboarder and loves creating new and exciting life experiences.

ABOUT THE AUTHORS

David Loshelder

Dave is the founder and owner of 3LG Solutions, LLC. His firm brings a unique blend of business experiences that provides a fresh look at personal and professional achievement. He is sought out as a speaker and author on personal effectiveness and change, interpersonal communication and leadership. Throughout his career, Dave has trained, coached, and counseled over 20,000 people to build stronger and healthier team cultures saving companies over 5 million dollars by producing highly productive teams.

Dave has spoken at many events and conferences. He is a certified Lean Six Sigma Black Belt, DISC Certified Trainer, Culture Change and Engagement Specialist and Personal Development coach. He also engages in consultations with companies and collaborates and develops process improvement projects and change leadership initiatives. Dave lectures to corporations, associations, civic groups, and universities about personal achievement, communication and leadership.

Dave is also the author of three books: *The MindCoach System*, *Take Care of #1* and *Protect Yourself*. He received his B.A. from Pennsylvania State University and M.S. at Duquesne University. He is also an avid martial artist and holds a 3rd Degree Black Belt in the sport of Judo.

CONTACT INFORMATION

For more information about

The MindCoach System

Visit:

http://www.mindcoachsystem.com

Email us at:

info@mindcoachsystem.com

Visit us on social media:

Instagram

https://www.instagram.com/mindcoach_system/

Facebook

https://www.facebook.com/mindcoachsystem

Twitter

https://twitter.com/MindcoachS

YouTube

https://tinyurl.com/y7leewgs

MINDCOACH SYSTEM PROGRAMS

MINDCOACH PERSONAL TRAINING

Do you have difficulty staying consistent and on track to achieving your goals? Do you lose motivation and get discouraged and feel like quitting? If this is you, then we have a solution to help you jump over your problems. Your personal coach will take you through The MindCoach System and keep you on track to help you reach your goals and life at a higher level. Sign up for our MindCoach Personal Accountability Coach today. Contact us at: info@mindcoachsystem.com.

MINDCOACH MANAGEMENT TRAINING SYSTEM (MMTS)

The MindCoach Management System trains managers on how to quickly become genuinely aware of your employees' personal dreams, goals, and perspectives and seamlessly integrates these passions into your company's mission. What this means is you will be able to communicate and motivate your employees on a deep meaningful level, they will feel happier and more appreciated, and you will see all aspects of your company's culture and financial performance improve. Contact us at: info@mindcoachsystem.com.

MINDCOACH MASTERMIND

Join a peer-to-peer mentoring group of high-achieving professionals. Exponentially increase your chances of success by accessing the knowledge and resources of others. Empower your dreams by surrounding yourself with a team that cheers you on and helps you reach your peak potential. For more information, please email us at: info@mindcoachsystem.com.

BECOME AN AUTHOR

Did you ever dream of becoming an author? The MindCoach System offers you the opportunity to become the author of your own book! By using The MindCoach System, you will take your expertise in your niche to the next level. Pair your talents and skills with The MindCoach System. If you always dreamed of becoming a published author, contact us at: info@mindcoachsystem.com.

MINDCOACH CERTIFICATION PROGRAM

Our certified coaches learn the nuances of The MindCoach System and provide support to individuals and organizations that want to play life at the highest level. This certification course will arm you with The MindCoach System tools, tactics techniques and strategies to coach others to their full potential. For more information, contact us at: info@mindcoachsystem.com.

MINDCOACH AFFILIATE PARTNER

Earn a part-time or full-time income by becoming an approved sales affiliate for The MindCoach System book, services, and related products. We offer a myriad of ways to earn money by assisting in the promotion and sale of our services to groups and organizations. To learn more about how to become an affiliate, please email us at: sales@mindcoachsystem.com.

SPEAKING ENGAGEMENT

The MindCoach System trainers offer presentations to corporations, associations, civic groups, and universities about personal achievement and leadership. For more information, contact us at: info@mindcoachsystem.com.

MINDCOACH PRODUCTS AND APPAREL

Visit Our Online Stores:

http://www.mindcoachsystem.com/

MindCoach T-Shirts, Mugs, Posters, & More

LEADERSHIP ACCELERATOR CERTIFICATION COURSE

Leadership Styles Accelerator will reveal the top ten dynamic styles of leadership to help you become a great leader.

You will learn:

- Powerful time-tested leadership practices that will make you stand out among other leaders
- Why learning and developing many leadership styles will arm you with the power to positively influence and motivate anyone under your command
- How to become more proficient and masterful at using and learning multiple leadership styles
- When to implement a particular leadership style and match it with the appropriate situation
- How to inspire and motivate people in your business, organization, and community to get measurable results

In just 14 days, you will show more confidence, have greater influence, and grow more fully in your own leadership journey.

This self-paced professional leadership development course is designed for current and aspiring leaders

To access the Leadership Accelerator course visit: www.mindcoachsystem.com

Contact us for the discount code at info@mindcoachsystem.com.

DISC PERSONALITY ASSESSMENTS

Discover how to take the guesswork out of interacting with others with the DISC Behavioral Styles Assessment!

"90% of the stress we experience in relationships is due to NOT understanding someone else's behavior style."

Your personal and organizational success depends on effective communication skills and the ability to connect well with others. <u>SO, WHY TAKE THE CHANCE AND GUESS?</u> The DISC will give you the knowledge to build relationships, team cohesiveness, and overall effectiveness within your organization.

More Effective Communication + Better Teamwork = Increase Productivity & Profit

You will learn how to...

- Motivate other people
- Communicate more effectively with others
- Become a better leader, communicator, parent, or team member
- Build more productive and deeper relationships with others
- Get results from your interactions
- Have less stress and more fun when you work with people

For more information about personality profiles, assessments and team building sessions contact us at: info@mindcoachsystem.com

OTHER BOOKS

by

David Loshelder

Take Care of #1

Protect Yourself: Top 10 Lifesaving Self-Defense Techniques

NOTES

www.ingramcontent.com/pod-product-compliance
Lightning Source LLC
Chambersburg PA
CBHW072002110526
44592CB00012B/1173